gene ——— perret

BUSINESS HUMOR

Jokes & How To Deliver Them

Sterling Publishing co., Inc.
New York

*"We need humor as much as we need any other kind of
sustenance in our daily lives."*

David Graves

Revision edited by Jeanette Green

Library of Congress Cataloging-in-Publication Data

Perret, Gene.
    Business humor : jokes & how to deliver them / Gene Perret.
        p.   cm.
    Rev. ed. of: Using humor for effective business speaking, © 1989.
    Includes index.
    ISBN 0-8069-9904-7 (alk. paper)
    1. Business—Humor. 2. Public speaking. I. Perret, Gene. Using
humor for effective business speaking.   II. Title.
PN6231.B85P485   1998
818'.5402—dc21   98-21161

1   3   5   7   9   10   8   6   4   2

Published by Sterling Publishing Company, Inc.
387 Park Avenue South, New York, N.Y. 10016
© 1998 by Gene Perret
Portions were previously published in
Using Humor for Effective Business Speaking © 1989 by Gene Perret
Distributed in Canada by Sterling Publishing
% Canadian Manda Group, One Atlantic Avenue, Suite 105
Toronto, Ontario, Canada M6K 3E7
Distributed in Great Britain and Europe by Cassell PLC
Wellington House, 125 Strand, London WC2R 0BB, England
Distributed in Australia by Capricorn Link (Australia) Pty Ltd.
P.O. Box 6651, Baulkham Hills, Business Centre, NSW 2153, Australia
Manufactured in the United States of America
All rights reserved

Sterling ISBN 0-8069-9904-7

*To my brother, Fran, who's a very funny guy . . .
but enough about his golf game.*

Contents

Foreword

Gene Perret writes humor, teaches humor, and he lives humor. He writes it because that's how he earns his living. He teaches it because it's fun. He lives it because he believes in it.

The first time I heard Gene speak was about ten years ago. He was giving a seminar on humor to an audience of professional speakers. He claimed in his opening that he didn't have a momentous message for any of us. Marketing wasn't his forte. He couldn't teach us how to get more bookings. Time management confused him, and his desk and office were hardly fitting samples of organization.

He said, "I told my wife I'm going to travel some distance, I'm going to work very hard, and no one's going to learn anything. I don't know if I can do it. She said, 'Sure you can, Gene. Just remember our honeymoon.'"

Here was a respected comedy writer inviting us to a laugh at his wife's friendly put-down. Here was a humorist using humor to teach us how to use humor effectively.

We laughed and we listened. We learned that a clever use of humor can capture and captivate an audience. We were all speakers; we all had a message. But a message is useless unless we, the speakers, get people to listen and to remember. That was Gene's message that day.

That's also the point of this very special book. In these pages Gene is reminding all of us that if we have something worth saying, it should be worth listening to, also. Humor is one of the tools that can grab and hold an audience's attention.

Perret is worth listening to. When he talks about comedy, the best in the world listen. Bob Hope has been performing comedy for over 60 years, yet he says, "When I need some extra special material I call on Gene. He's my trouble shooter."

You'll find him worth listening to, also, because he practices what he preaches. His sense of humor translates to the written page. The lessons are worthwhile, the substance is there, but it's delivered in an entertaining, anecdotal style. Again, it's the humorist using humor to teach humor.

I've been a friend of Gene Perret's since we first met after that speaker's seminar. We've shared the platform a few times, and we've exchanged speaker's and writer's war stories many evenings. Gene lives what he preaches. Humor is not only part of his life; it's his way of life.

His writing is delightful; his speaking is entertaining; most importantly, he's fun to be with.

You'll enjoy spending time with him in the pages of this book, and you'll learn much about communicating with humor.

Here's one of his anecdotes that's not in this book, but it tells you how Gene feels about humor. It's a story Gene is very proud of, but only shares with friends. I'm sharing it with you.

Gene had been asked by Bob Hope to write some lyrics for a song. He didn't feel that was his strongest writing skill, but he finished the assignment. Gene says:

"When I handed Bob Hope the pages, he asked, 'Is it brilliant?' I said, 'Bob, if I could write brilliant song lyrics, would I still be writing comedy?' Hope looked me in the eye and said, 'Yeah, you would, Gene. You would.'"

Bob Hope was right. Gene's still writing comedy, still speaking with humor, and still teaching humor. I'm glad.

Og Mandino
Author/Lecturer

PART I

The Business of Humor in Business

"One horselaugh is worth ten thousand syllogisms. It is not only more effective; it is vastly more intelligent."
H. L. Mencken

CHAPTER ONE

The Power of Humor

There is a speech that is delivered every single day of the year. In fact, it's delivered thousands of times daily. It's an important speech, yet hardly anyone listens to it. It's the safety instructions that flight attendants must deliver before each flight.

Some of us don't listen because we don't want to admit that something might go wrong with this flight. Let other people on other flights listen—the flights that might have problems. Some of us seasoned travellers are too arrogant to listen. We know all there is to know about planes and exits and what to do and when to do it. When this discourse begins, we smugly snap open our attache cases, take out yellow pads and begin our personal work. We want the other passengers to know that our business is more important than any life-saving procedures might be.

Others don't listen because they're too busy trying to stuff their sixth carry-on bag into the overhead compartment—on top of my neatly folded suit jacket.

These safety instructions are probably the most universally ignored lecture in history.

I was on a flight recently, though, where everyone listened and heard the instructions. The flight attendant introduced herself and her assistants over the intercom. Newspapers rattled, briefcases popped open, bags were pounded into non-existent spaces in already filled overhead compartments. Not a head snapped forward in attention.

"There may be 50 ways to leave your lover," the attendant said, "but there are only five ways to leave this airplane." There were a few chuckles and people glanced around from behind the open lids of the briefcases. We were confused. Had we boarded a plane or a nightclub? We listened to make sure.

The attendant continued. She was determined to have us know just where the exits were. "Even if you know where these exits are, please turn around and locate the one nearest you. We noticed when you boarded that there are some pretty good-looking men and women on this flight—you know who you are. We think the people sitting behind you deserve to get a look at you, too." Everyone proudly turned around and chuckled.

We were all caught up in her monologue now and wanted to hear more.

"In preparation for take-off," she said, "please return your seat backs to their full upright, locked, and most uncomfortable position. Later you may lean back and break the knees of the passenger behind you."

She was getting solid laughs now, and people who normally travel coast to coast without communicating with any person or thing besides their pocket calculator, were smiling, nodding, and actually talking to one another.

The flight attendant went on to explain where our oxygen masks would come from and how we were to operate them. She told us that we could fasten them exactly the way the flight attendants were now demonstrating, "Except," she added, "when you put yours on, you're allowed to muss your hair."

"Those of you travelling with small children, or just people acting like small children, should put your masks on first."

This young lady forced us to listen to a message that we didn't want to hear. She had conquered "white knucklers" and seasoned travelers. She overpowered us with humor.

I thought there were tremendous lessons in this demonstration. First of all, she did get us to listen. She harnessed a reluctant audience. Her message was a potentially life-saving one. She got us to hear it. Second, she livened up her own act. Probably, she was bored giving this same talk over and over again, but with these new twists, she added a little gusto. She seemed to relish the laughter, and in fact, when she finished, the applause. Third, she created a more pleasant atmosphere. People were laughing, kidding with one another and enjoying the safety instructions.

It carried over into the flight. We were all more pleasant than usual with the flight attendants and with each other.

That's the power of humor that business people shouldn't overlook. Wouldn't all of us love to be able to get reluctant customers or employees to listen to our important messages? Wouldn't we pay gladly to have them pay attention when they don't want to? Wouldn't we offer almost anything to have them listen and hear our side of a story when they've already made up their minds—knowing they have nothing to learn from us? This young lady did it; why can't we in business do it?

Wouldn't we love to enjoy our tasks as much as this airline employee enjoyed hers? Wouldn't it be nice to get the reception she got? They actually applauded safety instructions.

Wouldn't we be more valuable if we could create the same kind of climate in the office that this woman created on the plane? It was a long flight and her talk lasted only a few minutes, but what an impact those few minutes had. She improved morale on that aircraft, and it endured.

Let's look at another example. In this illustration, there was some money on the line—quite a bit of money. It was a court case that involved a Mississippi river barge that accidentally rammed and damaged a newly built railroad bridge over the river. The railroad was suing for recovery.

The barge owner disputed the railroad's right to interfere with navigation. Because the case had such far-reaching consequences, the railroads loaded the courtroom with their best and highest paid attorneys.

The case was complicated, long, and tedious. The railroad lawyers presented logical evidence that impressed the jurors. The barge owner retained a single lawyer. In his closing argument he admitted to the jury, "My learned opponents have presented an impressive case. There is no question that they have their facts absolutely right. But they have drawn completely wrong conclusions."

The jurors laughed heartily. Then they adjourned and returned quickly with a verdict in favor of the barge owner.

What happened? The losing attorneys wanted to know, too. They asked the country lawyer. His name was Abraham Lincoln.

As the story goes, Lincoln confessed that he ran into the jurors at lunch that afternoon and told them a tale about a farmer whose young son came rushing up to him. "Pa," the boy said, "come quick. Sis and the hired hand are up in the hayloft. She's got her skirt hiked up and he's got his overalls down. If you don't come quick, Pa, I think they might pee all over our hay." "Son," the farmer said, "you've got your facts right, but you've drawn a completely wrong conclusion."

Probably all of us saw, heard, or at least read about another example of the power of humor. Some feel it may have gotten a man re-elected to the Presidency of the United States.

When Ronald Reagan campaigned for re-election, age was quite a concern among the voters. He would have been, at the end of his second term, the oldest President ever to hold the office. His first debate with Walter Mondale didn't help him. Most analysts thought he did badly. He looked tired; he looked old.

Mondale couldn't attack too viciously, because he didn't want to appear to be the heavy who was ousting a man from his post because of age. He didn't really have to attack too strenuously anyway. Reagan's tired, confused appearance was more telling than any remarks Mondale could have made.

The pressure was on Reagan to bounce back in the second presidential debate. He had to respond to the unasked age question. He got his opportunity.

One of the questioners said, "Mr. President, you already are the oldest President in history, and some of your staff say you were tired after your most recent encounter with Mr. Mondale. I recall that President Kennedy had to go for days on end with very little sleep during the Cuban missile crisis. Is there any doubt in your mind that you would be able to function in such circumstances?"

The journalist was really asking, "Are you too old to be President?"

Reagan said, "I want you to know that I will not make age an issue in this campaign. I am not going to exploit, for political purposes, my opponent's youth and inexperience."

Even Mondale laughed. The audience laughed and applauded. The line was quoted on the front pages of most newspapers the next day as the turning point in the debates.

Humor can have that kind of power.

Understand, though, that humor isn't always the dramatic, quotable line that makes the morning paper and alters history. If it does, and it can, fine. But it's still a powerful everyday tool even if you don't have professional writers turning out your quips. A good sense

of humor—and a wise use of humor—is mostly an attitude. It's a commonsense way of looking at yourself and the world around you.

One last caution—this is a book about humor and how it can be an executive tool. The examples I use are naturally examples of humor. And it doesn't take much. Lincoln, Reagan, and the other people mentioned in these pages, didn't go around doing jokes during the entire day. These short, isolated examples show not only how well and how wisely they used humor but also how sparingly.

Noel Coward said, "Wit ought to be a glorious treat, like caviar; never spread it around like marmalade."

These pages don't want to turn promising executives and competent business speakers into comedy club performers. You're not on the podium to get laughs, applause, and critical reviews; you're there to make a point.

Humor, though, can be a powerful ally in getting your message across. It's an ally that many in the business world neglect or ignore. It has power and it should be used.

Where does this power come from? What can humor do for a speaker and how does it do it? Let's take a look.

CHAPTER TWO

What Humor Does
for the Speaker

The speaker seems to have all of the advantages in a meeting room. All the chairs are aimed in his or her direction. A lectern is provided for notes. Perhaps a podium even elevates the speaker a foot or so above the audience. No one else has a microphone. Yet the speaker has one drawback—he or she is horribly outnumbered.

Most talks begin as an adversary confrontation. That's not to say that each speaker walks into an auditorium and greets a lynch mob, but there is a dash of suspicion in most crowds. And a touch of resentment. The audience asks itself, "Who are you to presume to teach me anything?" "How come you're up there in the spotlight and I'm down here in the cheap seats?"

Of course, with well-known performers, that suspicion might not exist. The listeners know them and their credentials. They've accepted their expertise. But if you're an ordinary business speaker, you may still have to prove yourself. You have to win the audience to your side. You may not always convert them to your point of view, but you should at least convince them that you have the right to offer them a point of view.

Humor can help accomplish this conversion in several ways.

1. Humor generates respect: I've made a few military trips into war zones with the Bob Hope Show. One incident that happened at sea off the coast of Beirut, Lebanon, illustrates how respect affects the power of a speaker. We had just finished a show and our cast and crew were milling about waiting for a helicopter to carry us back to our home ship, the *USS Guam*. Our work was done for the day, so this was R & R—social time, party time—for us. We were guests of the military, but none of the military discipline had rubbed off on us.

The officers were trying to maintain some order so that when our helicopters landed on deck, we could quickly load and evacuate. Our crew was competent and knew what they were doing, but they didn't line up two-by-two in alphabetical order. They relaxed and chatted until a job had to be done; then they did it quickly and efficiently.

We had one "weekend soldier" who was assigned to this trip with us. He worked at NBC and was also an officer in the Marine Reserves, so he seemed a perfect liaison officer to accompany us. He wasn't.

Carried away with the bars he had earned during his weekend tours of duty, he appointed himself the reformer who would bring order out of our unregulated chaos. He jumped up on some loading crates. His spit-polished jumping boots reflected the sun; his neatly pressed camouflaged fatigues screamed military authority. He barked in his fiercest marine drill instructor voice, "I want the following people to report to me front and center on the double . . . ." Then he yelled out the names of a few of our crew members.

It was such a jarring display that our chatting ceased. Everyone turned and looked and listened—for just a second. Then seeing who it was, we turned back to our chatter.

He grew red-faced barking orders, but no line of personnel ever formed in front of his make-shift podium. We certainly heard him. He bellowed so loudly that the Shiites in the Druze Mountains probably heard him. But no one listened.

Then choppers approached the ship. Our staging supervisor issued a few quiet orders and cameramen, electricians, sound men, all moved with orderly precision. We loaded our gear and personnel, lifted off, and flew back to our ship. We listened to one of the men because we respected him and ignored the other.

Of course, we knew both people. We had been living with them and working with them for several days. They had established their credentials—good and bad. A speaker must establish that respect within the first few minutes of meeting the audience.

Authority doesn't do it. The first gentleman had the military demeanor and the rank. It meant nothing. Authority, in fact, may be a hindrance. So you're the boss. That just means that you want something from this crowd. Sure you want us to work harder, improve your standing with your superiors, and perhaps get you promoted.

Besides, your audience may be convinced that management is the least competent part of the work unit. Don't many executives rise to their level of incompetency? Aren't the people who really know what should be done working in the mail room or as janitors?

That's how your audience might think.

The TV show M*A*S*H used to highlight this attitude each week. Every officer above the rank of the stars, except for Colonel Potter, who was somehow exempt, was an imbecile. So were the people in Washington. Every person of any authority was an idiot. It's a false notion, but a notion that exists. It's a notion that a speaker, as an authority figure, must overcome.

Humor is an excellent way of gaining respect. You may not have a problem with this. Your work record and the business decisions you've made may already have established you as a person who should be listened to. That's great. However, any time you face a new, unfamiliar audience, you have to overcome that sliver of doubt. Humor can help you do it.

Humor that encapsulates the situation and defines it is the best type for earning that respect. It tells your audience quickly and concisely, "I know what the situation is, and I know you know what the situation is. Now I have something to say that's worth listening to."

2. Humor gets the listeners' attention: I've heard some people say, "My message is too important to include humor." Wasn't Ronald Reagan's message important? He wanted to become President again and had invested millions of dollars in the effort. Wasn't Lincoln's message critical? He needed to win an important and potentially costly case for his client.

If you feel your message is truly important, you want to have it heard. Why not use every method available to make sure people get it?

I like the example of the woman who resorted to whimsy to get a reply from her grandchildren at college. The parents complained that the youngsters never wrote. Grandmom said she'd send a letter and get a reply within a week. She did. She received a pleasant page of happy chatter from the campus, ending with, "And Grandmom, you did mention that you were enclosing a check, but there was none in the letter."

People love to be entertained; they love to laugh. Have you noticed at trade shows and conventions how the booths that draw the biggest crowds offer some sort of gimmick—a magician, a game, or something like that? Fun attracts people.

At parties, people glance with envy at the crowd in the corner who are laughing and enjoying an entertaining conversation.

The friends you value most, on reflection, are often the ones that you have the most fun with.

It's human nature; we all love a good time.

Sometimes at seminars or conventions I will speak at concurrent sessions. I'll be speaking in banquet room A, while banquet room B hosts a seminar on "Zero Based Budgeting," and room C has a lecture on "Personnel Problems of the '90s." I always instruct my audience: "Laugh loud and hard even if you don't like some of the jokes. Let's make the people in the other rooms think *they* picked the wrong session to attend."

Every speaker should be aware, too, that just because people are in the room, staring up at you, with notebooks open on their laps and pens poised, that doesn't mean they're paying attention. Minds can wander easily and they leave no tracks. Those bright blue eyes in the third row that are staring up as you speak may be wondering what dress to wear to the awards banquet tonight. The guy in the fourth row may be looking at the lady in the third row and wondering if he should ask her to dance after the awards banquet no matter what dress she wears.

I remember the ultimate in inattention once when I was working on a story conference for the television show, *Three's Company*. As producer, I had brought a difficult story problem to two of the executive producers for their solution. They pondered for a while, then one of the execs popped up enthusiastically with a possible answer. He said, "How about this idea?" Then he acted out the entire scene, complete with business, props, and pratfalls. It took him about four minutes and considerable energy to get his idea across. Finally, he turned to his partner and said, "So . . . what do you think?" His partner said, "I'm sorry, Bernie. I wasn't listening."

When you include some light-hearted humor and entertainment in your talk, listeners perk up. They table their daydreams about this afternoon's golf-tourney or tonight's cocktail party in favor of a little fun right here and now.

I recently heard a speaker in California who lectured on the same day that a mild earthquake shook the area. She mentioned that there is a theory that our animals, if watched closely, can give us hints about when a tremor is due. She said, "If I had paid attention to my pets I would have known an earthquake was coming. They gave me a clue. Last night the two dogs took the family car and drove to Arizona."

Her audience listened pretty well.

3. Humor holds their attention: None of us are creatures who are designed to stay on one subject too long. We tire of it; we look for variety, diversions. While you're speaking about business trends and expectations, your audience may be wondering where you bought that tie and if it's really silk.

Listening to a talk, even a beneficial one, is work. The mind of the listener has to cooperate with the speaker. It has to absorb, analyze, and judge the material. It's almost like studying. The audience eventually hits a saturation point. When that happens, they need a recess.

That's the value of a short coffee break at work. It's why you forget about the problems at the office and take in a movie once in a while. It's why a boxer needs a one-minute rest between rounds. It's a chance to recover and regroup.

A speech may be momentous, but it's also exhausting. To keep an audience attentive, you have to give them a little ice-pack on the back of the neck between rounds. You need to offer a little refreshment so they can maintain their stamina.

You don't need much. Just a little break—maybe a funny quote, or a one-liner. An anecdote might do it. Then you can get back to the work at hand, knowing your audience is still with you.

I remember one speaker giving us a short break by saying, "I'm telling you the truth here. Sometimes the truth is painful. Like when a young mother showed me her new young baby—the most unattractive baby I had ever seen—and asked me if I thought it was cute. What could I say? The truth would hurt. So I said, 'He looks a lot like his father.'"

4. Humor can clarify obscure or complicated issues: Abraham Lincoln was a polished story-teller. It was a skill he honed as a lawyer travelling through the Eighth Judicial Circuit. He was probably the first President to use humor as a political and executive implement.

As he was campaigning for President his advisors sometimes implored him to use stories more. Anecdotes were effective, they argued, and could win him support and votes. Lincoln said, "I do not seek applause . . . nor to amuse the people. I want to convince them."

His anecdotes were not only convincing, but they also saved valuable time. He said, "I often avoid a long and useless discussion by others or a laborious explanation on my own part by a short story that illustrates my point of view."

Good humor has to be clear. It has to appeal to the listener and be understood. It must be easy to recognize and identify. The truth and reality of it have to be apparent. If not, the listener simply "doesn't get it."

That clarity, recognition, and understanding, though, work in reverse as well. Understanding the principles behind the joke can help a person understand your point of view.

I remember in the presidential debates of 1984, Mondale said to one of his adversaries, "Where's the beef?" That was a catch phrase from a popular TV commercial at the time. Mondale's quote got tremendous press and served him well. The people listening to the debate understood his point at once. He was saying, "You have all these policies, but there's no substance to any of them. Where's the beef?"

I remember a simple line that cut through a lot of technicalities, euphemisms, political diversions, and much else. It was during the Vietnam conflict. We had fighting men there, but they weren't supposed to be fighting men because it wasn't supposed to be a war.

The guys who were there were as uncomfortable as if it were a war. People were shooting at them, which reminded them of a war. To them, it looked like a duck, quacked like a duck, and waddled like a duck, but it was not allowed to be called a duck.

When Bob Hope came to entertain, he began his monologue by saying to the troops, "Hello, Advisors."

They were just two simple words, but the fellows in the audience knew what they said.

As executives, we often have to explain policies that are difficult to accept. It's not that the listeners can't understand, but the situation behind them may be too tangled to unravel. Especially in those cases, a wise selection of humor can illustrate the salient points.

I once listened to a manager give a pep talk to a group that had let down badly. Production had to improve or the entire line would be dropped and layoffs begun. The talk was factual, but also threatening. What had happened—and why—were beyond the scope of the lecture. But the manager made his bottom line point emphatically. He said, "I'm not saying all these things because your jobs are on the line. I'm saying them because mine is."

5. Humor helps your audience remember your points: No message is worth anything if the listeners leave it in the meeting room. Your audience has to take that message home with them, or at least, back to the office. Humor can help your listeners do that in two ways: First, it helps them remember what you said and, secondly, it helps them recall it when they need it.

Let me give you an example of what I mean. I had a friend once who was an incurable name dropper. Since we were all in show business, we would tell stories about stars we knew. My friend would always have a story about that same star after you told yours. It might not be a better story; it was just a story. It said, "I know that person, too."

When he was told that this habit was annoying, my friend accepted the criticism, but said, "I don't do it maliciously. It's just that I do know these people and your stories always remind me of another story." Then someone quoted Will Rogers's remark about a fellow he liked: "He's my favorite kind of musician. He knows how to play the ukulele, but he don't."

It made the point well, and it also served as a constant reminder. Each time my friend was prompted to tell a "topper" story, he remembered "not to play the ukulele."

Why is humor such a good reminder? Because good humor is fun, it stays with us. We always remember the good old days and forget the bad. Also, humor is graphic. A worthwhile story, joke, witticism, is not so much a collection of words as it is a picture in the mind of the listener.

That's why different people react to different jokes in different ways.

No two listeners paint the same mental image. Phyllis Diller's material has always been highly graphic. When she kids her husband's drinking, and she says, "Fang cut himself shaving this morning. He bled so badly his eyes cleared up," you can't help but form some sort of visual. You may see a man whose bloodshot eyes are gradually draining. You may laugh a bit louder if you picture the way you've looked on certain mornings. But you do form a picture, and pictures stay in our memory longer.

To illustrate this, here is a little experiment. I'll give you a list of ten 4-digit numbers. You can spend some time and try to memorize them, or you can estimate how long it would take you to remember them. Don't waste a lot of time on Part One of this experiment because it's Part Two that is enlightening.

Part One

Here are the numbers:

1. 3452
2. 7843
3. 9024
4. 7726
5. 8705
6. 2145
7. 3598
8. 4233
9. 4581
10. 3909

First, for Part One: if you did try to memorize those numbers, I'm sure it would take you some time, and you probably wouldn't remember them for too long. End of day, they'd be gone—certainly by tomorrow.

Part Two

For Part Two of this experiment, though, I'll give you another list of ten numbers, but I'll give you a graphic way of remembering them. I almost guarantee that you'll remember them easily. They'll remain with you all day, and probably tomorrow you'll be able to recall most of them, too.

Let's try it. Here are the numbers:

1. 1439
2. 1211
3. 4416
4. 5205
5. 1349
6. 2576
7. 6599
8. 5088
9. 5529
10. 2048

Before you start, I'd like you to memorize these visuals. They are picture words that rhyme with numbers, from one to ten. One is gun, two is shoe, three is tree, four is door, five is hive (a beehive), six is sticks, seven is heaven, eight is a gate, nine is a bottle of wine, ten is a hen. Memorizing those should take about half a minute.

Now, break down the four-digit numbers into combinations of two-digit numbers. For example, 1349 becomes 13-49 and so on. Then I'll give you pictures that suit the numbers. From that we'll paint a graphic picture that will remain in your head. The wilder and more bizarre the image is, the easier it will be to recall and the longer it will remain. Let's try it.

For number one, we picture a gun, but a unique gun—a blunderbuss. A person jumps out of a hiding place with the gun, but instead of threatening you, he forces you to take a vacation. The vacation signifies the number 14, for 14 days. So you picture yourself riding in a rickshaw around Hong Kong with Jack Benny. Why Jack Benny? Because he was always 39 years old. Hence, you get that image in your mind and you have the first number—1439.

Now (for two) we picture a large shoe, like the old lady who lived in a shoe. The door of the shoe opens and out rush the twelve disciples with numbers on their togas and helmets on their head. They're rushing out to play a football game. The significance? There are twelve disciples and eleven men on a football team. Hence, the second number is 1211.

Next is a tree (for three). Picture a pretty girl in an old-fashioned white dress swinging from a swing on the tree. However, she jumps up and starts firing western pistols. The guns are Colt-44's, and the girl is sweet sixteen. Therefore, the third image is 4416.

Four (door) is a pair of swinging doors to a western saloon. You walk through and start playing cards with a basketball team. The guys are so tall that you can hardly reach the card table. There are 52 cards in a deck and five men on a basketball team. Four equals 5205.

For five (hive), a black cat jumps out of a beehive and starts chasing some old westerners who are in the river panning for gold. It's a mad chase. The black cat is for the unlucky number 13, and the gold-panners are '49ers. Five equals 1349.

Next you picture a pile of twigs on a silver tray. The sticks represent six, and the silver tray is for 25, the silver anniversary. You hear faint music coming from the twigs. You move the twigs aside and see three tiny little men. They march around the tray. One plays the flute, another the drums, and the third proudly carries the American flag. They are the spirit of '76, representing the last two digits—76. Therefore six is 2576.

For seven you visualize the pearly gates of heaven. St. Peter has to open the gates quickly because an older gentleman with grey hair is coming through. He's being chased by an old-time train engine. The significance: The old man is 65, the traditional retirement age. The train is Engine 99. So, seven is 6599.

Eight is a beat-up old fence gate. You swing it open and discover a dazzling, gold piano. The gold represents 50, the golden anniversary. The piano means 88, the number of keys on the keyboard. Eight equals 5088.

Nine, you are drinking from a bottle of wine. You are sitting by the bottom of a roadway marker that reads 55. It's the speed warning by the side of the road. Along the roadway you see a bunch of down-and-out stockbrokers pushing apple carts. This represents the crash of '29. Therefore nine means 5529.

Finally, you see a very large hen (ten) walk into an open mine. In it a bunch of miners are playing pinochle. The miners represent the number 20, the last year you are a minor. Pinochle means 48 since there are only 48 cards in a pinochle deck. So ten is 2048.

I'm glad you persevered through this experiment with me. Test yourself, though. Ask yourself what the sixth number is. Do you remember what you visualized when you thought of a gate for eight?

You should be able to recall most of these four-digit numbers with little or no study—nothing beyond the brief reading of the paragraphs contained in the text. Notice what has happened. With crazy, zany, yet graphic word pictures I tricked you into a commendable feat of memorization. I got you to commit to memory 40 digits in sequence—something that you probably wouldn't do otherwise.

You can do the same for your listeners with graphic, funny, *memorable* illustrations. You can dupe them into remembering what they don't particularly want to remember—but you want them to. That's the power that a judicious use of humor can give a speaker.

This is, of course, a gimmick, but a serious one. Most memory systems are based on graphic visualization. Picturing images does enhance the memory.

Humor not only gives you a graphic image to help your memory, but it also gives you another idea to relate to. That aids recall also. For example, let me ask you if you know the square root of three. Do you remember the birth year of George Washington? I know both. I've remembered them since my sophomore year in high school. I couldn't forget them even if I wanted to. Why? Because some astute teacher once told me that Washington was born in the square root of three. That one remark enabled me to remember that Washington's birth year is 1732 and the square root of three is 1.732. What's even more remarkable is that I didn't know either one before he said that.

Can you name all five Great Lakes? I would always forget at least one until an instructor told our class that if we owned two homes we would remember them. That was a hint she dropped; we had to do the detective work on our own. Then one of us hit on the solution and probably none of us has forgotten it since. "Homes" is an acronym for the five lakes—Huron, Ontario, Michigan, Erie, and Superior.

If you want people to remember what you say, give them graphic stories to illustrate your main points. They'll stay locked in the mind longer. In fact, they're difficult to forget, just as you probably can't forget that a black cat jumped out of a beehive and chased some guys panning for gold. And the fifth number was 1349.

6. Humor can relax tension: A toy existed when I was a kid called the "Chinese Finger Torture," or something exotic like that. It was simply a cylinder woven from some fibrous material. You'd insert both forefingers into it and then discover that the harder you tried to pull them out, the tighter the fiber would bind together, locking your fingers in.

None of us, of course, stayed trapped forever (well, maybe one or two kids from the neighborhood, I don't know), but the principle is interesting. The more you resisted, the tighter it became. Tension in an auditorium is like that.

It's like when you make a social faux pas—say something you shouldn't say, for example—the more you try to cover, the more embarrassing it becomes.

Tension is a part of public speaking. It's especially prevalent in business meetings because existing tension is often involved in the reason for getting together in the first place. There are meetings to boost lagging production, meetings to lift failing sales figures, meetings to decide whether to go with product A or product B, meetings to decide whether Sales or Marketing was at fault in the recent fiasco, and so on.

Tension, if allowed to continue, can create a distraction for both the speaker and the listeners. The speaker can certainly be aware of it, intimidated by it, and affected by it. The listeners are thinking about the unresolved issue instead of listening to the message. So, it's best to confront it, face it head-on, and dismiss it. Humor is a very effective way of doing that.

I remember one of my first confrontations at work involved a new drafting technique that I introduced. The manufacturing representative resisted it—hard. He and I got to butting heads so furiously that our manager had to step in to resolve the issue. When he called us into his office, I was eager to prove that I wasn't at fault and the marketing rep was just as prepared to show that it wasn't his fault, either. Our manager stopped us cold.

"I want all of us to relax and work together on this problem," he said. "I'm the one who's at fault here. I hired both of you."

7. Humor can defuse an adversary's attack: I was playing a singles tennis match with a good friend one day when his wife and her girlfriend approached the court. His wife shouted, "Would you like to play mixed doubles?" My heart sank. It wasn't a sexist reaction, believe me. I enjoy good mixed doubles play, but these ladies weren't at our level of tennis. I was looking forward to a good, competitive singles contest.

While I mentally struggled to find an excuse that would be believable and inoffensive—but effective—my friend simply shouted back, "Life is too short."

The women laughed and went to the next court for some singles of their own.

My heart had skipped a beat. The "fight or run" adrenaline had kicked into my system; my mind went blank; my tongue swelled up. I became a helpless, slithering wimp. Yet he used just a dash of wit, and the problem was deflected.

Humor can have a paralyzing effect on an opponent, or perhaps it would be more accurate to say that it can allow an opponent to have a paralyzing effect on himself. It's a passive form of combat, so to speak.

Some forms of martial arts use that strategy. They allow an adversary's weight, force, strength, and momentum to be used against him. Rather than oppose the attack, you flow with it. That's the secret of humor as a defense mechanism.

A good example is Ronald Reagan during the 1984 Presidential campaigns. As we mentioned before, age was a major issue. It wouldn't go away because his opponents wouldn't let it go away.

The Reagan camp could have countered with fact-filled rebuttals, because many studies indicate that age doesn't affect mental capacity. However, these arguments would only have invited counter-argument and the troublesome issue would have remained center stage.

Reagan's response was to de-activate the issue with humor. He did age jokes on himself as often as he could. When his opponents tried to bring up the issue, it was dead—deflated. Reagan had done it—himself. He effectively joked the annoying argument out of existence.

Here are a few of the gags he did on himself:

Some people reminded Reagan that if he were reelected, he would be 76 years old when he left office. Reagan replied,

"Well, Andrew Jackson left the White House at the age of seventy-five and he was still quite vigorous. I know because he told me."

Speaking to the Gridiron Club, Reagan noted that the organization had been founded in 1885. "How disappointed I was," he said, "when you didn't invite me the first time."

Reagan once told a group of doctors, "We've made so many advances in my lifetime. For example, I have lived ten years longer than my life expectancy when I was born—a source of annoyance to a great many people."

8. Humor can get results: Some arguments can go on forever. As kids in Philadelphia, my buddies and I used to debate endlessly which was the better team—the Athletics or the Phillies. Was Robin Roberts a better pitcher than Bobby Shantz? Some 35 years later, we can still get hot under the collar during these discussions.

Business disagreements can last almost as long. The basic questions can get fogged in by egos, personality clashes, departmental restrictions, and who-knows-what-all. Competent business logic surrenders to pettiness and nothing gets resolved.

Humor can help clarify these situations. The brightness and innate logic of humor can often bring a muddled situation into distinct focus.

We once had a small, but lingering strike where I worked. Most of the issues had been reasonably resolved, but the union and management negotiators now were waging a power struggle. Neither one would compromise, so the company and the workers suffered because of their stubbornness.

Each day the union issued a bulletin "explaining the facts." It didn't explain any facts at all. It just slung mud at the company negotiators. It was so obviously sarcastic and slanted that even the union members were embarrassed by it.

Then the company team would issue a rebuttal bulletin. It would out-sarcastic the union sheet. Now the union members would rally behind their besieged officials.

The union would then publish another page or two and the problem would continue see-sawing.

I was the supervisor of the striking workers, so the union team invited me to the strategy sessions. They asked my advice. I told them a story about a talk I had heard a college football player give. He was a very mediocre offensive lineman, but he had played a great game against a consensus All-American that weekend. He told us about it:

"If I tried to block this guy out of the play, he would just toss me aside and rush into the play. I wasn't good enough to control him. So, I started blocking him *into* the play. Then he'd toss me aside and run away from the play and leave a big hole for our runners to go through.

"He was too smart to put up with that for very long. When he caught on, I would sometimes block him into the play and other times I would block him out of the play.

"It got to where he would just guess, and half the time he guessed wrong. When he guessed wrong and ran away from the play, I'd just let him run."

That's how the kid had an outstanding day of football against a far superior ball-player.

I told our company negotiating team that the union, with their ill-conceived personal attacks, were running the wrong way. When they did, we should just let them run. Replying in kind was uniting the union members against us.

When our General Manager convinced the negotiating team that they should swallow their pride and not respond to each attack, the union membership forced their negotiators to accept what was actually a reasonable settlement in the first place.

9. Humor can motivate and inspire: Wit has such a well-defined logic, making its points forcefully and clearly, that many excellent speakers also use it to motivate.

John Heisman, the Georgia Tech football coach after whom the Heisman trophy is named, would make his point very demonstrably at the beginning of each football practice season. He'd hold up a ball and announce, "This is a football. It's an elongated spheroid, inflated with air and covered with an outer layer of coarsely grained leather. Heaven help the first man who fumbles it."

Knute Rockne, the famed Notre Dame football coach, was reportedly a bombastic halftime orator. His locker room pep talks were classics of motivational fire and brimstone.

At one game in which Notre Dame was being decidedly outplayed, the team trudged into the locker room at half-time and waited. They knew their coach was going to lean into them heavily, and they were prepared for a loud harangue. But Rockne never showed up. They waited and wondered, but still no coach. Finally, just before they were called back out to the stadium, the coach opened the door and said, "Oh, excuse me. I was looking for the Notre Dame football team."

Notre Dame won the game.

Finally, here's a little story that doesn't fall into any of the other categories. It was humor that certainly came too late to motivate or inspire. However, I enjoyed it so much that I think it's worth ending the chapter with.

John McKay coached the University of Southern California one day in a losing cause. He must have felt his players let him down, because after the game he went to the locker room and said, "The team bus leaves in half an hour. Those who need showers, take 'em."

CHAPTER THREE

The Dignity of Humor

Let's flashback to our entertaining flight attendant from Chapter One. You remember, the young lady who used a few jokes to get us all to listen to her safety instructions. Let's get annoyed at her.

After all, this is a message that is mandated by the FAA. It's not to be treated lightly. It's not to be ridiculed, played with, or made sport of.

There are many people who could be incensed at this employee's actions. She defiled the sanctity of a serious message. She did a disservice to the passengers who have a right to a message free of capricious editorializing. She diminished the dignity of all flight attendants, most of whom are serious, hard-working employees, dedicated to the comfort and safety of their customers.

Boy, are we pissed off.

Suppose, though, there had been an emergency. Would you have preferred to have had a dignified, august lecture on safety, or one that every passenger heard and absorbed?

Let's look at some of the possible complaints against this humorous approach and respond to them.

"It makes light of the instructions." Well, it didn't make light of them. This young lady kidded the passengers. We all enjoyed it when she said we were a handsome crowd, and we got a kick out of turning around so the folks in the back could see us. We thought it was funny when she kidded our travelling companions by saying, "If you're travelling with children or people acting like children." She teased her own airline, or more accurately all airlines: seatbacks *are*

uncomfortable when they're in their full, upright, and locked position. She poked fun at her own colleagues by pointing out that when they put on an oxygen mask, they didn't get one strand of hair out of place.

She kidded many things, but not the instructions. They were important to her. They were the reason she was forcing us to listen.

"She was being disrespectful." To whom? To what? The passengers enjoyed it—the overwhelming majority of them. We enjoyed it so much, that the good feeling continued throughout the entire flight.

Her airline must have approved of it. I've heard other flight attendants give similar safety lectures since then, so I'm positive the authorities have given their blessing.

The FAA couldn't object. They want this lecture heard, and it was heard.

"I don't have much confidence in a person who would stoop to such shenanigans when she should be taking her job more seriously." Quite the opposite: This young lady took her job seriously enough to force a group of reluctant listeners to pay attention to her. She knew we had never listened before, but we listened today. She captured us.

She knew enough about the situation, her job, and us, to get done what had to be done. I felt quite secure travelling with her. If a serious problem did arise, I believe she would have handled it with the same confidence and sense of humor. Isn't that the kind of image we're all looking for?

There are those who criticize all humor. Laughter and fun belong at parties and in nightclubs, they say. Others feel that any comedy, except on the professional stage, is undignified.

Certainly, I don't mean to give carte blanche to all forms of humor. I'm not suggesting that anything that gets a laugh is appropriate in your office or in your business speaking. Certain forms of comedy are annoying anywhere and some are unsuitable for executives. We'll discuss them later in the chapter. It's the resistance to levity of any kind in the business world that is worth analyzing here.

Many people have that prejudice. Laughter in the office is wrong, they feel. "We are there to work, and work should not be fun."

Recent studies are showing that managers have begun to appreciate the productive qualities of humor in the office. With a sense of humor, workers get along better, promote morale within the office, can accept managerial direction better. A sense of humor is high on their priorities in searching for managerial talent, too.

Why should humor be suspect in the office? Well, humor is generally honest. And sometimes that is hard to take.

There's a story about a woman on a train with her infant. A passenger looks at it and says, "That's the ugliest baby I've ever seen in my life." The mother is infuriated. She physically attacks the transgressor. Finally the conductor breaks up the fracas and tries to calm everyone down. He says, "Sit down, lady. Relax and take it easy. I'll get a banana for your monkey, and everything'll be all right."

Because humor is so incisive and so relentlessly rational, many people don't want to permit it to affect their thinking. "I've made up my mind," they insist. "Don't confuse me with facts." A manager who is convinced that his image is proper, but his competence is suspect may insist on perfect decorum in his office. "Let's stick with style because exposing substance could get me canned."

Those who are not afraid of the truth are not afraid of humor.

Someone once told me that "the truth will never hurt you." I don't buy that. Anyone who has ever seen my tennis game knows that telling the truth about it can seriously hurt my ego.

How about someone who wants to be a great football player, but just doesn't have the skills? Doesn't it hurt to inform him?

A young lady may want to be a famous fashion model. She simply doesn't have the bone structure. Isn't it painful for her to discover this?

You want to be the CEO of your firm. Isn't it distressing to discover that you probably never will be?

Sure, all of these things hurt. Assuming, though, that they're all true, isn't it better to find them out and redirect your ambitions rather than lead a fruitless life? It's not the truth that goes on hurting; it's the resistance to the truth.

Sure, my tennis game is lousy, but I continue to have fun. I just play lousier players who haven't yet realized how terrible they are.

Once I accept the reality of my tennis game, I can have fun with it. My friends can kid me. I enjoy that. I once was playing net in a doubles match and my opponent hit a shot right past me, down the alley. It was a clear winner. I pointed my finger at him in mock retaliation. "I hold a grudge for a long time," I said. He answered, "The way you play tennis, I imagine you'd have to."

The first requirement for a solid, dependable, there-when-you-need-it sense of humor is a confident self-image. If you can look at yourself honestly and like what you see, you can allow others to look at you critically. You can have a sense of humor about what you see and what they see.

I was going to give a talk about this once and I prepared a statement like this: "As I look around this room, I know that I'm better than half the people in this room, and not as good as the other half." At first I thought it was a pertinent, meaningful line; then on reflection I realized it was dumb.

There is no measure of who is better than whom. Is Pete Sampras better than me because he hits the tennis ball harder, or am I better than him because I can write more funny lines faster? Is the big guy in the third row of my audience better than me because he's built better, or is the guy in the 15th row better than both of us because he's got a higher IQ? What basis do you use to evaluate the worth of individuals?

I'm not better than any of the people in my audience nor any worse. We're all just different. We all have pluses and minuses that total up to an individual. When you're happy with that individual, you can be justly proud of the pluses, and have a sense of humor about the minuses.

Let's quickly see how a solid self-image helps your sense of humor and helps you in the long run. You're at a party or in a club and some stranger calls you "Hook-nose." Now this angers you. It angers you mostly because he's right.

So, what do you do? You challenge him. Why? Because that's another one of those misconceptions that we've come to accept. A macho man doesn't allow himself to be belittled. He fights for his dignity.

Suppose, though, you have a powerful, yet honest, self-image. Sure, you have a hook-nose. So did George Washington. In fact, they put his on the one-dollar bill. They carved it into Mt. Rushmore, right near Abraham Lincoln who had a pretty big schnozzola himself.

Yeah, you've got a hook-nose. It's the same one your wife fell in love with. Your kids aren't going to throw you out of the house because of it. That beak of yours may just add the right touch of character to your features.

Even if you consider it a liability, it's still only a part of the picture. You've presumably got so much else going for you that it overshadows this drawback. People like comedian David Brenner even kid themselves about things like that. Brenner says, "When I was a kid, my nose was so big I thought it was a third arm."

You can take the hook-nose and assign it either a plus or a minus value. That's up to you. It's not up to some stranger. Therefore, what that person says should have no effect on your personal evaluation. If you have a strong enough self image, it won't.

Some of our greatest leaders show us how to have a sense of humor about ourselves. Lincoln used to tell a story about meeting two elderly ladies while he was out riding one day. He frightened them a bit. The one woman said angrily, "Sir, you are the ugliest man alive." Lincoln said, "I can't help that, M'am." She said, "You could at least stay home."

There's also the story about the time Churchill reportedly had too much to drink. A woman at the party chided him, saying, "Mr. Churchill, you're drunk." He replied, "And you, Madam, are ugly. But tomorrow morning I'll be sober."

Some feel that levity, if not the arch-enemy of dignity, is at least a threat to it.

Well, they took Abraham Lincoln seriously. They took Will Rogers seriously enough to ask him to run for President. He refused. He was a comedian; not a politician. I think he enjoyed more getting his laughs on purpose.

They take Bob Hope seriously, too. He has dined with kings, queens, presidents, prime ministers, heads of state. He is sophisticated, urbane, dignified—and funny.

Again, the conflict between humor and dignity arises when we try to present a false veneer as genuine.

I used to play golf on the public links in Philadelphia many years ago (my golf was worse than my tennis). Several of us were on the starting tee bright and early one Saturday morning. It was so early, in fact, that the first hole was shrouded with morning mist. You could only see about the length of a mediocre tee shot.

As we crowded around, waiting for our startup time to be called, a foursome approached the first tee. They were gorgeous. They had all the proper equipment and their golf clothes were expensive and matching. They were too splendid for our lowly public course.

Then they teed off. The first shot went about 70 yards. The next went about 30 to the right. They just kept walking along the fairway swinging at the ball. We all watched stunned as they each took about 4 slices at the golf ball before mercifully disappearing into the mist.

When they were out of sight, we laughed uncontrollably. They were dressed for golf, but they weren't prepared for golf. You see, the costume is not the ability. Dressing like Tiger Woods doesn't improve your backswing. Looking like the Masters Champion doesn't get you from tee to green in regulation. In fact, it can make you look even more absurd.

The accoutrements of dignity are not dignity. There are those who would look dignified, and there are those who have dignity. They're not always the same.

Mortimer Levitt, founder of the Custom Shops and a very wealthy man, said of class, "Arriving in a Rolls Royce is not class. That's the accoutrements of class. Real class is how you treat your chauffeur."

Let's take a look at the forms of humor that might be harmful to a business speaker.

1. Slapstick or physical humor: This generally doesn't belong in the business speaker's repertoire. Milton Berle used to get a lot of laughs and big money dressing up in women's clothes and walking on his ankles. I don't think the manager of sales should open an employee meeting with this shtick.

2. Gratuitous insults: Many professional comics rely on the insult joke. Don Rickles is probably the outstanding example. His insults are obvious. There are others who do more insidious insulting and for no good reason. We writers call this gratuitous. There is a joke in an insult, therefore you do the insult to get the joke. It's not prompted or motivated by any logic.

Business leaders should avoid this type of humor at all costs, because it shows a lack of sensitivity. One manager I worked with years ago used these types of jokes constantly. He'd insult other managers and other departments. We'd all wince when we heard him. It wasn't that we disagreed with his conclusions; we just hated his presentation. It was cruel, vicious, and unfair. It showed us that he didn't think things through before speaking.

3. Put-down humor: This dangerous form of wit says to an audience, "I'm better than you, and don't you forget it." It boasts of being superior—whatever that is—richer, more sophisticated, at a higher management level, whatever. It inflates your own standing and deflates your audience. It may get laughs, but it won't win anyone over. It antagonizes people.

4. Sarcasm: This is another dangerous, insidious form of humor. It pretends to be wit, but it's really viciousness in disguise. An audience can feel the difference.

Will Rogers said it best: "If there's no malice in your heart, there can't be none in your humor."

The acid test here is what you intend to accomplish with your wit. If you're trying to make a point, you can be caustic. If you're trying to wound, don't.

Note: None of the above rules out insult humor. When this is used well, and wisely, it can be a powerful tool. There are ways to insure that your insults are harmless—more fun than fang. We'll talk about those in a later chapter. For now, though, realize that humor is a powerful tool. It shouldn't be used to hurt.

---

5. Questionable taste: This covers material that might be considered dirty, ethnic, or sarcastic, as well as hurtful insult humor. Remember that the humor you use reflects on you, just as the clothes you wear do. It's never worth offending anyone with your wit. The best rule of thumb is: if you're in doubt, don't.

6. Humor that contradicts your personality: If your humor really is a reflection of you, everything you say, even in fun, should be consistent. Why? Because you're using humor as a business tool. It serves no purpose to confuse your listeners. They would wonder which is the real you—the serious one or the witty one. There's no confusion if you're consistent.

7. Humor that contradicts your philosophy: As an executive, as a business leader, you have a philosophy. You have a set of ethics that you adhere to. Any humor you use should be consistent with that. Humor used judiciously can gain respect for any speaker. But humor that contradicts your thinking can wreck people's respect for you. Be sure that what you say in jest is what you would say seriously. People are going to hear *everything* you say. What you say with humor may be heard even more clearly than the rest. Be sure it's what you want to say.

In working for Bob Hope and other comics, it's amazing how much funny material they just won't do. They won't permit themselves to. Even for professional funny people, image is important.

As a youngster I used to listen to a radio personality. He had a kiddie show and I was among his biggest fans. One night, he mentioned my name and told me to look under the sofa for a birthday gift. I did, and sure enough there was a watch there. I was thrilled and mystified. I had no idea that my parents had called in and told him what to say.

One night I listened to him as he said a sincere good-bye to all of us youngsters; then he said something else. He didn't know the mike was still live. He said, "Well, that should take care of the little bastards for another day."

That was the last time I ever heard him on radio.

CHAPTER FOUR

Overcoming the Fear of Humor

When I was a writer on *The Carol Burnett Show*, we had a guest star who wasn't too pleased with the sketch that we had written for him. He was a respected, talented dramatic actor who had a hit detective series on the air. He was also a fine gentleman—very professional, and a delight to work with. He just didn't care for this particular sketch.

He respectfully requested that we replace the sketch, or at least, replace him in it. But Carol, the staff, and the rest of us thought it was hilarious and persuaded him to stick with it a little longer. He did, but his heart wasn't in it.

He rehearsed with little gusto, simply reading the lines—no enthusiasm, no flair, no emotion. Rehearsals went poorly.

On tape night, this gentleman was depressed. He didn't want to go out there and do this sketch, but by now it was too late to avoid it. When he got his music cue, he walked onto the set, still reluctant. He was determined to do this piece of material bravely before a live audience, endure their indifference, and then walk around backstage with an unspoken "I told you so" written across his features.

He delivered his first line and it got giant laughs from the audience. The crowd bought the concept, thought it was funny, and roared.

This gentleman's eyes were a sub-plot in themselves. At first they were diverted in shame from the audience. At the sound of the laughter, they lifted up in disbelief. He looked at the audience openly, as if to reassure himself that they weren't laughing at someone running naked up and down the aisles. When he saw that he was a comedy hit, his eyes lit up. They sparkled. He was rejuvenated with new energy, and he performed the rest of the sketch like a marvelously broad burlesque ham. He was magnificent, and he had the greatest time of his performing life. He had discovered comedy.

Many people fear humor. And with good reason, too. In 1833, British actor Edmund Kean was near death. A friend at his bedside whispered comfortingly, "How are you doing?" Kean's famous answer was: "Dying is easy; comedy is difficult."

When I give seminars to speakers and comedy writers, I hear this echoed constantly, though less dramatically.

"I can't do comedy."

"I just can't tell a joke."

"I can never remember jokes."

"Every time I try to be funny, I fail."

I sympathize with these complaints, but I don't believe any of them. Oh, I believe that the people are sincere. I believe that they've tried humor and failed. But who hasn't?

In any humor seminar I give, people ask, "What are some of the common mistakes people make in using humor?" My first reply is, "They quit too soon." Beginning writers abandon the joke line too quickly. They stop writing the routine before they've exhausted the possibilities. Speakers jump ship after the first abortive attempt.

None of them are giving humor—a difficult art form—a fair chance.

Golf is not easy, either. Yet, people don't take a few swings and say, "I can't play this game,"—"I can't master the swing,"—"I've tried to break 90, but just can't do it." Not at all. They take their lessons, get their weekend starting times, and continue to play. And they get better.

They could make the same strides with humor if they would give it a fair chance.

Let's analyze a few of those objections.

You can't do comedy? Of course you can. Everybody can. You can't do it the first time out, maybe, but neither could you hit a golf ball correctly on the first swing. You couldn't drive the first time you sat behind the wheel, either. Hell, you had trouble walking when you first started, too.

You can't tell a joke? Don't be so critical of yourself. If you can make a point with logic, if you can "sell" your point of view to clients or fellow workers, if you can inspire and motivate people with your lectures, you can tell a joke.

Our guest star on the *Burnett Show* could work the emotions of an audience with his dramatic training. Those same skills worked when he tried comedy. It surprised him, but it didn't surprise us. We knew from dealing with comedy week after week, that more people can handle it than realize they can handle it.

Remember, though, that this man destroyed several rehearsals with his negative approach. You, too, can influence the results with your attitude. Delivering humor with "I just can't tell a joke" in the back of your mind, hurts. Try to go into each effort "full out." Hold nothing back and you may discover with delight, as our reluctant comedy guest star did, that the audience won't hold back either.

You can never remember jokes? So what? Who says you have to? When you deliver a speech, you generally have time to prepare it, don't you? Well, that should give you ample time to research a dash of humor, too.

You're not being challenged to a duel of wits with Jerry Seinfeld. You don't have to toss out rapid-fire insults like Don Rickles. You needn't ad-lib in a constant, funny stream-of-consciousness like Robin Williams or Jonathan Winters. You simply need a clever quote, a cute aside, or an amusing anecdote to illustrate your main points.

Also, you are permitted to use notes. So why worry about remembering jokes?

Every time you try to be funny, you fail? This reminds me of the reply Victor Borge gave when an interviewer asked if he had played piano all his life. Borge said, "Certainly not. I'm not dead yet." Maybe every time you tried to be funny, you failed—until now. Now is when you're going to start trying it, get better each time, and eventually learn how to use humor effectively.

If you're really honest with yourself, you have to admit that you can be entertaining. That's as important as anything else you'll learn in the following pages.

One final encouragement, though, before we move on. Any fear of humor you have must be tempered with the reality of what you're trying to do. Edmund Kean was right; comedy is difficult. But you who are reading this book are not trying to become comedians. You're not stepping to the podium to do a 90-minute nightclub act like Bill Cosby. You don't have to do a solid hour of one-liners like Bob Hope. You are simply trying to augment the power of your message with humor. There's a tremendous difference.

Why are people afraid of humor?

Humor is powerful: Like electricity, fire, or any source of power, humor can do harm. I've been hurt by it a few times. In one company I worked in a department that was a bit off the wall. We were known as the "zanies" of the plant, and I don't say that with pride. In one of my monologues I did a little routine about it. Jokes like, "Our supervisor left the office for a while the other day. By the time he got back, we had let all the sand out of the sandbox."

I delivered this routine in front of fellow workers and representatives of management. Afterwards, my supervisor came to me and said, "You've just killed my career at this plant."

I'm not sure I destroyed his career, but I did hurt him with that routine. It was ill-advised, not thought out, and it did harm. It offended him, first of all, and it probably did reflect on his record.

Yes, humor can hurt. However, that needn't produce fear; it should generate respect. There's a difference. Normal people don't fear electricity; we respect it. We don't stick knives into toasters, we don't repair lights or outlets without first switching off the power, we don't replace burned out fuses with a penny. But we're not terrified of turning on the light switch, and we don't cringe each time we change channels on the TV.

As with any potentially harmful force, we need to learn what can cause the damage and then deal with it. The hurt from humor can stem from either of two sources: malice or ignorance.

Humor can be used maliciously. That's what children do when they taunt others. That's what we can do when we use comedy or sarcasm to antagonize others. That's what union and management were doing in those strike flyers I mentioned earlier.

The remedy is simply to vow not to use humor as a weapon.

Ignorance is a little more precarious. We generally know when we're being malicious; we don't know when we're ignorant.

There is some ignorance that we'll never be able to do anything about. Knowledge simply isn't available to us. For instance, I visited a factory and did a humorous routine about the age of the building. It was quite old; everyone knew it was ancient; and they had kidded themselves about it often. But the gags didn't play. Why? Because the employees had just gotten word—and it wasn't yet available for public knowledge—that the factory would be shut down because it was effectively obsolete.

The "harmless" one-liners now had a painful barb to them, but I had no way of knowing what had happened.

Generally, though, our ignorance is remediable. When I kidded my supervisor, I should have realized that it would paint him as incompetent. I didn't. That was my fault.

The solution is to think through any humor you use. Learn to hear it through the mind of your listeners. If this humor you're using were said about you, or your work, or your associates, would you be offended by it? If you would, don't say it.

Humor is not easy: My manager always reminded me that "simplicity is the product of thought." Good, effortless, natural flowing humor is the end result of lots of hard work.

I have worked with many of the top names in professional comedy and I can guarantee that effort goes into their humor. I have worked on staff for a performer who might deliver 20 comedy lines on camera. We wrote over 3000 to get those 20. I've been at meetings where one line needed replacing before a sketch could be taped. The writing staff might stay at the typewriter until 2 o'clock in the morning in order to have the line ready for the next day's taping. I've written ad-libs for comedians where we had to write a different line for all possible contingencies. Would the guest star say this? We'd answer with that. Would the guest star not say this? We'd reply with a different line. Would the guest star not show up? We'd have a line for that, too.

Humor requires homework and effort. We have to research, write, and rehearse our delivery. People like Robin Williams and Jonathan Winters seem to be able to do it spontaneously; the rest of us, even the top professionals, have to work at it. To try to do it without that effort, dooms our comedy to failure.

But wait a minute! If it's that difficult and requires so much effort, why should we even attempt it? Especially since we're not pros.

First of all, because it is a powerful tool. We've already discussed the merits of humor in business communication. A good executive is not going to reject such enormous benefit simply because it requires some work.

Second, the response to humor is immediate and honest. You've probably been in clubs where a singer performed badly. Still, at the end of the number, the audience politely applauded. They can't be that gracious with bad comics. They can't force laughter.

The flip side of that, though, is the benefit for the speaker. When humor works—when it hits an audience—the listeners can't disguise that either.

Many professional business speakers insist on evaluation cards. They want to know exactly how the audience rated their performance. Professional humorists don't care about evaluation cards. Anybody who is doing humor knows exactly how the audience rates that performance. The reaction can't be hidden and it can't be faked.

So when using humor well and wisely, you control the audience instead of vice-versa. That's a powerful implement to have with you at the podium.

Third, and we've touched on this already, you don't have to get big, sustained laughs. You're not trying for a career on the comedy stage. You're only looking for a touch of wit to strengthen your speaking. So, do expect to work at your humor, but that work should be proportionate to the amount of humor you'll be using.

For those of you who do have a genuine fear of humor, here's a step-by-step remedy:

1. Go gradually: Try to conquer your fear in small doses. Don't load your next speech with stories, one-liners, anecdotes, and quotes. Be satisfied with one amusing moment. Aim for just that. When you're satisfied that you can get that chuckle when and where you want it, then you can go for two, three, and eventually as many as you like.

2. Research one good piece of material: Make a concerted effort to find just one good laugh-getter. It can be a quote, a one-liner, or a good story. But read, research, ask other speakers what they've had luck with, and get one piece of material that *you* are convinced will work.

3. Rework the material to your satisfaction: Rarely will you find a piece of humorous material that you can do "as is." In other words, if you find an anecdote in *Reader's Digest*, it won't be in your words. It will be in *Reader's Digest* words. You now have to work with it until it sounds comfortable coming from your lips. Change the speech patterns. Change the "he says-she says." Make it sound like you.

Usually, it's just a matter of changing something from a literary form to a more conversational style. But it should be *your* conversational style.

4. Rehearse your delivery: Now that you've rewritten your story so that it indeed sounds like *your story,* you have to learn to say it like it's your story. That takes rehearsal time. Say it aloud. Hear how it sounds coming from you. Repeat it so often that when you begin to tell the story, the rest of it falls off your lips.

I once worked with a major motion picture star. For a while he was the biggest box office draw in the world. When he came to our first script reading, I was stunned to find that he was almost illiterate. He couldn't read the script as quickly as the rest of the cast. It was painful to sit through rehearsal. Yet, when the cameras were turned on, this gentleman recited each line flawlessly. Because he had so much trouble reading, he rehearsed with added diligence. That's why he performed so well.

So, whether you fear humor or not, it won't hurt to practice it to perfection.

5. Tell your story often: Now try your story with an audience. Tell it to friends. Tell it to anyone who will listen. You'll get the honest feedback that you need.

Each time you tell it you may learn a little more about the telling of it. You may change the way you tell it. In any case, you'll get better and better as you get more and more confident in the telling.

If you follow these steps with just one piece of material (no matter how tiny—it may just be a quotation from some famous person), you'll learn the process. It will become easier when you repeat it with another piece of humor and another. Gradually, you'll build up a repertoire and overcome that unnecessary fear.

CHAPTER FIVE

Humor and the Business Executive

I especially need a sense of humor because there are times in my life when I do dumb things. To paraphrase some anonymous humorist, "I'm quick to laugh at myself, if only to beat somebody else to the punch."

A medical group hired me as a luncheon speaker for their convention in Tahoe. They arranged my flight into Reno where they had me picked up by limousine for the hour ride to the convention hotel. However, right before my luncheon speech, they asked if they could make alternate arrangements to get me to the airport for my return flight. The limo, they said, was too expensive.

I didn't mind losing the limousine, but I did have a tight connection at the airport because of another speaking engagement. They said they had arranged for a shuttle to the airport.

Now I was concerned. I had used the shuttle once before in Tahoe and it stopped anywhere and everywhere. One time I remember we stopped at a supermarket to pick up a young lady who had just finished her weekly shopping. She had two children and several bags of groceries with her. When we reached her house, the rest of us on the shuttle helped her unload both kids and groceries. Because of my tight schedule, I thought the shuttle was out of the question.

My hosts had no alternate plans, and I lost my temper. "Forget about making any plans for me," I said. "I'll get to the airport myself. This is too important to me, and you folks don't seem to be concerned about details. I'll get to the airport myself, thank you."

Despite my irritation, the luncheon talk went well. At the end of it,

I asked if there was anyone going to the Reno airport immediately after lunch. A doctor volunteered to drive me there, and we had a pleasant ride.

I arrived with very little time to spare, thanked the doctor, and rushed to the check-in desk. "Am I on time to make this flight?" I asked. The girl behind the counter smiled and said, "You'd be in plenty of time except for one thing." "Except for what?" I barked. "Except you're at the wrong airport."

I was at the Reno airport; my return flight was scheduled to leave from the Tahoe airport, which was only a ten-minute drive from the hotel. I could have comfortably made it on the shuttle even if we did have to help a few people with their shopping bags.

In Tahoe I only made a fool of myself before strangers. The rest of the time I act dumb with my family. That's much worse; you have to see them every day.

The trumpet fiasco started when one of my children began to tire of music lessons. Like a good parent, I insisted on a practice session. Reluctantly, my offspring obeyed and we listened to scales being played badly on the trumpet. Each note had a ring of resentment to it.

When the practice time mercifully ended, my youngster asked me for help getting the trumpet back in the case. The mouthpiece was jammed onto the instrument.

I tried to pull the thing off but couldn't. We both tried to pull, one holding the horn, the other tugging on the mouthpiece. It wouldn't budge. The more I struggled with it, the angrier I became. I figured in a display of spiteful revenge, the ten-year old had purposely jammed this thing into the trumpet.

I got out my tool box. I put a thin piece of metal into the trumpet from the bell and tried to bang the mouthpiece out from the inside. I tapped it with a hammer, but still couldn't loosen that damned mouthpiece.

I banged a little harder. When I looked to see if I was loosening the part that was wedged in, I saw that the piece of metal was tearing through the side of the instrument. Now I couldn't get the piece of metal out.

So I inserted another piece of metal, a long file, to unwedge the first piece of metal. I lost that into the trumpet and couldn't get it out.

Now I was not only mad at my youngster, but at my own stupidity, and at whoever designed trumpets in the first place.

I became irrational, frightened my child, and did a lot of damage to an innocent horn.

When my temper quieted down, I realized that I now had to go to a music store and act nonchalant while asking a man to repair a trumpet with a sizable gash in its side and 4 or 5 pieces of metal and tubing wedged inside it. I hoped he wouldn't ask.

He didn't. He just stared at me in wonder. Then he explained what he would have to do. He'd have to weld a new part onto the trumpet to replace the torn metal. The instrument would be usable, but not equal in quality to the original. He'd also have to disassemble the horn to see if the offending metal had done any internal damage. The whole repair job would cost about $150. I said that would be all right.

I wasn't happy with my embarrassment, nor with the expense. The worst was yet to come, though. The repairman then said, "First of all, I'll have to get a mouthpiece pull to get this thing off." With a simple little device and perhaps 20 seconds of effort, he pulled that mouthpiece off just like taking a stick of gum out of the wrapper.

With just a touch of common sense and a phone call to a music shop, I could have saved myself $150 and some respect.

I might get a little more sympathy in this last anecdote of the trilogy, but not much. After a supposedly routine medical exam, I found that I had a problem that required heart surgery. As a precaution until the surgery, I had to wear a patch on my body with medication on it that was absorbed topically, through the skin.

I wasn't much fun to be around during that time. First of all, I was angered that I had a problem; I was comparatively young, ate well, kept myself in good shape with a reasonable amount of exercise and just couldn't understand why I needed repair work. In other words, "Why me?" Second, I hated this medicine. It had annoying side effects, and it was awkward. No matter where I taped it onto my body, it would come loose.

At dinner one evening I was my usual unbearable self. I told my family, who were more understanding than they needed to be, what was bothering me. "I hate this patch. My body is covered with hair, and no matter where I tape it, it comes loose." My daughter, who had had enough of my complaining, said, "Why don't you tape it on top of your head?"

What a terrible thing to say to her bald father. She won't be allowed out of her room for another two years.

In each of these three stories (and I don't mean to imply that I've only done three dumb things in my lifetime—I may have done as many as six), I lost my sense of humor. In each of these tales, I not only acted foolishly, but also inefficiently.

Had I sensed the humor in these situations, I would have remained calm. Had I remained calm, I would have reacted more rationally, with more logic. Had I reacted more logically, I would not have done the dumb things that I did.

A sense of humor affects our decision-making mechanism; that's one of the reasons why it's important for business people.

These stories I've confessed to didn't cost me that much. Perhaps some embarrassment and a $150 repair bill. In the business world, though, actions like mine could be terribly expensive, both in actual costs and in harm to one's career.

Humor and logic are closely aligned—probably more closely than we realize. I remember I was shocked many years ago when I first began to write for Phyllis Diller. Phyllis, as you know, does many bizarre, zany, outlandish, crazy lines about herself, her children, her husband, and whatever. Yet, I sent her one joke that was illogical. She sent it back to me with a note reading, "Honey, if it ain't true, don't send it to me."

We can exaggerate a premise, distort it, view it from an oblique perspective; but basically the humor must be true.

Good logic, and consequently sound decisions, must also be based in fact. As our Abraham Lincoln story (page 13) points out, you can draw wrong conclusions from valid facts. Correct conclusions must be founded in truth.

What's the connection between humor and logic? I feel that a sense of humor has three prerequisites:

1. the ability to *see* the facts as they really are.
2. the ability to *recognize* the facts as they really are.
3. the ability to *accept* the facts as they really are.

We seem to lose our sense of humor when any one of these prerequisites is missing. We forget to laugh at ourselves when we're confused—either we don't know what's going on, or we don't know why it's going on. Or sometimes we just wish it weren't going on. We refuse to accept it and wish it would go away, happen to someone else, or happen next week when we'll have more time to cope with it.

Let's look back at my three stories at the start of this chapter. In the first, I didn't even realize there was a problem. I didn't know I was going to the wrong airport. I could have known; it was written clearly on my ticket. I just assumed I would leave from the same airport that I arrived at.

If I had known that the airport was only ten minutes from the hotel, there would have been no reason to get upset with my hosts. They had planned both my arrival and departure adequately. They were perfectly right in realizing that it would be unwise to pay an expensive fee for a limousine that only had to go a few miles down the road. I probably could have walked to the airport and arrived in time. There was no problem.

But, I didn't know the facts. I didn't see the real situation, and I caused myself a lot of unnecessary trouble.

In the second instance, I had the facts. I knew the mouthpiece was stuck and had to be unstuck. But I didn't recognize—and didn't bother to find out—that the problem was easily correctable. My anger blinded my reason and I transformed a minor annoyance into an expensive calamity.

I didn't recognize the reality of the situation.

In the third story I just refused to accept the facts. I knew I had a problem that needed treatment; I just didn't want to admit it to myself. I didn't want to give in to this discomfort without causing some discomfort back. I chose to be a grouch so that I wouldn't be the only person suffering unfairly. Everyone around me would suffer unfairly, too.

The condition didn't warrant this much self-pity. Clear thinking would have shown that all of us will have problems from time to time.

It was now my turn. The medical solution was not a simple or easy one, but neither was it the melodramatic event that I was making it.

I lost my sense of humor about myself and refused to accept the facts that were.

In each case, what I did was dumb. You see, there's another angle to this idea of seeing, recognizing, and accepting the *real* facts. When we do, they are generally less disastrous than the unreal facts.

When we reject the real facts, we have to create new ones to replace them. Usually, we manufacture situations that are much worse. I created a scheduling problem that didn't exist. I battered a petty problem into a $150 repair bill. I worried an ordinary operation into a life or death fantasy. My sense of humor was turned away and replaced with fantasized, manufactured, non-existent problems.

Let me off the hook for awhile and imagine a situation that you may have experienced and see how forgetting your sense of humor can cloud your commonsense reactions.

You're driving along a freeway at a safe, comfortable rate of speed. That's probably about five to ten miles above the speed limit. You have a pleasant station on the radio and you're making good time.

Suddenly, a speeding car swerves into the lane in front of you. He didn't force you off the road or anything. He simply was going very fast and cut ahead of you.

Now you're angry. I mean really angry. You don't even hear the soothing melody on the FM station. You don't care that you haven't been delayed at all. You're still on time for your meeting. All you care about is that this guy insulted you. He demeaned your driving. He implied that you weren't going fast enough for him. He as much as said that you were driving like a sissy.

Consequently, you have only one option. You have to speed up, chase this automobile, cut him off, and prove to him that he should never again challenge your driving skills.

So you do.

You lose your sense of humor. You abandon logic. You react irrationally and chase this anonymous driver, risking your own life and the lives of others on the road in your reckless pursuit.

I know that story is not too contrived, because it has happened to most of us. It has happened to me often.

Let's study how a sense of humor—a sense of logic—seeing, recognizing, and accepting the real facts would have helped.

If you had seen the facts as they are, you would have known that this was a reckless driver. At least, it was someone who drove with more abandon than you're comfortable with. There are plenty of drivers like that on the roads. Some reports say that almost half of the drivers you pass on the highways are under the influence of something—either alcohol, drugs, or common, ordinary impatience.

Rather than being surprised and angered at this encounter, you might have been prepared for it. If you saw the facts clearly, you might have driven, for your own safety, as if all the drivers who share the freeways with you are reckless.

Then you might have recognized that this was not personal. This person didn't cut in front of you to show that you weren't half the driver he was. He didn't want to belittle you. He simply wanted to get where he was going—perhaps faster than he should. He really wasn't interested in tossing down the gauntlet and challenging you to a "drive off."

Even if he were, so what? Your self-worth doesn't depend on outdriving every nut with a driver's license.

And you might have recognized rather easily—with just a moment of reflection—that you wouldn't want to risk your life and property for a clown who will turn off at some exit, never to be seen by you again.

Finally, you would accept the fact that these erratic drivers will always be with us. They'll exist regardless of new laws, stricter regulations, more careful surveillance, and whatever lessons you and I might teach them.

Your life would be calmer and safer if you just permitted them to drive on out of your life.

Let me cite another example of how a sense of humor generated sound logic:

In 1973, I was on the phone with Bob Hope the day his home, then under construction in Palm Springs, caught fire. At first, neither one of us realized how serious it was. He got a call on a second line and said, "There's a problem at the house. I'll call you back."

Before he called back I learned from news reports that the entire roof had burned. It was a costly and serious fire, although, thankfully no one was injured.

When Bob Hope called back he said, "Did you hear about the house?" I told him I had. He said, "Do some jokes about it."

I did the jokes. I wrote things like:

"It's a terrible feeling to wake up one morning and find out the black cloud hanging over Los Angeles used to be your home in Palm Springs."

"I think the fire was caused by a mix-up with the builders. I definitely ordered the place medium rare."

"Everything was fried to a crisp except the water bed. That was boiled."

"Of course, a huge crowd gathered. My house doesn't work without an audience."

"In front of all those people my house was destroyed. Now it knows how I felt in vaudeville."

But Hope's reaction puzzled me. Faced with a setback like this I would have been angry or depressed. Maybe I would have moped around searching for sympathy, or I might have gotten vicious and attacked the builders or the fire department or just kicked my dog. Who knows?

So I asked Hope, "How can you joke about this? How can you take it so calmly?"

His answer was enlightening. He said, "It went up awfully fast. I'm glad it happened now rather than after we moved in."

Because he reacted with a sense of humor—he reacts to almost everything with a magnificent sense of humor—his analysis was perfectly logical.

Those attributes that comprise a sense of humor are the same ones that enable an executive to make sound business decisions. You have to be able to see the problem, analyze it to find the cause, and then, perhaps most difficult of all, be able to accept the problem and its consequences.

As an example, suppose one of your new sales representatives is just not meeting his or her quotas. That's a problem for you as a manager. However, it's a bigger problem if you don't see it. That's why all good executives have a reporting system—a measuring unit—so they can see potential problems developing.

Okay, suppose you see that this new sales rep is well below quota. What do you do? Fire that employee? Well, maybe, but wouldn't it be wise first to find out why the sales are so low? It might not be the salesperson's fault. It may be your fault. Maybe the documentation you released is offensive in this particular region of the country. Maybe one of the plants that used to buy most of the product has shut down or relocated. It could be that the last salespeople, knowing they would be leaving the region, sold at a heavy discount rate in order to sop up all of the profits beforehand. The new sales rep can't sell in an area that's been saturated.

Whatever the reason, a good executive needs to investigate before making a decision.

Then you have to be realistic enough to accept your own findings. If it is your documentation, you have to change it. If it's the sales rep, you have to make that move. You can't wish either one were better than it really is.

Let me offer one final example of this theory of seeing, recognizing, and accepting. The medical problem that I talked about earlier was a cardio-vascular problem that required heart surgery. My cardiologist told me that I was lucky. For many people, their first symptom is their last. They don't survive a first heart attack. I asked why that was. He told me there were three reasons:

First, some of them don't get any warning symptoms. There is no pain, no pressure, no discomfort of any kind. They simply don't see that they have a problem.

Second, many people experience a shoulder or chest pain, but misread it. They assign it to too much tennis, or too much snow shoveling, or any number of other reasons. They feel the symptom, but they don't recognize it.

Third, some have the symptoms and immediately know that they're serious. They know it's their heart warning them of trouble. Yet, they don't accept it. They say, "I'm too young to have a heart attack," or "It'll go away if I watch my diet," or "I'm strong enough to endure this for a while," or "I'll check with my doctor later when I'm not so busy at work."

Unless they see, recognize, and accept the symptoms, they make a very costly bad judgment.

A sense of humor is a sense of reality. It's knowing and accepting the truth. Both good humor and good judgment are based on reality—on truth.

A good use of humor makes you a more effective businessman,

which in turn improves your self-image, which in turn improves your sense of humor. It's the opposite of a vicious cycle!

You can get this cycle going merely by appreciating the power and the benefits of humor in your everyday life, and especially in your business. Learn to lean on it when you need it the most—that is, when you have problems.

That sense of humor clears your mind. It leaves it free to appreciate the true facts. That vision permits you to make logical judgments. There are more benefits of humor in the workplace. How can we overlook them?

Will Rogers' comments usually were as philosophical as they were funny. (Have you noticed how often, in talking about humorists, the words "wit" and "wisdom" are linked together? That's what this chapter is about.) I'd like to paraphrase one of his lines in summing up business judgment. "A committee was formed to study the high cost of doing business. They turned in their report which said, 'We find the cost of operating our business very high and we recommend more funds to carry on the investigation.'"

CHAPTER SIX

Humor Is Not Necessarily Jokes

A friend of mine has a promiscuous sense of humor. He not only laughs readily at practically anything, but he laughs loudly and vigorously. I would like to multiply him one thousand-fold and take him on all my speaking engagements as my personal audience.

Despite that glorious, hair-triggered laugh, I rarely tell him a joke. Why? Because I'm dreadfully afraid that he'll try to tell me a joke in return.

Then his infectious laugh becomes a turncoat. It switches from friend to foe. He giggles and guffaws so much throughout the telling of the story that it not only becomes three times as long, but also unintelligible. You don't hear words; you hear random syllables interspersed through giggling.

He can take a delightful joke and make the retelling of it just slightly less painful than root canal work.

Bob Murphey, a popular and delightful humorist, once told an audience of speakers, "The first thing I look for in any room that I speak in are the 'exit' signs." He continued, "I'm not afraid of fire. I've been a volunteer fireman in my town for many years and I have a healthy respect for fire, but I don't fear it. I'm not afraid of a major catastrophe. Most hotels are prepared for that sort of thing and a minimum of common sense ordinarily will rule the day. So I'm not afraid of catastrophe. What I am deathly afraid of is the guy who grabs me by the lapel, gets right up close to my nose, and says, 'Have you heard that one about . . .'"

There *are* people who can't tell a joke. Every time I speak to speakers about humor I hear the complaints. "I try to tell jokes, but nobody laughs," "Everybody recommends opening with a joke, but when I do it ruins the rest of my talk," "I can't tell a joke." Then they tell me a joke and I believe them.

People like this shouldn't tell jokes (at least, not yet. The condition is real, but not always incurable.), but they can still use humor.

The point is that humor doesn't always imply jokes, stories, or anecdotes. Wit is not limited to those stories that begin with "These two guys went into a bar . . ." Humor is an attitude; it's a style; it's a flair.

Not all funny people, even professional funny people, are joke tellers. Bob Hope is not a storyteller. He does do jokes, but they're one-liners. He rarely tells an anecdote, a story-type of joke. Myron Cohen, on the other hand, was a professional comedian who told nothing but stories. Cohen would come on stage and proceed from one anecdote to the next without even a segue. With his Jewish dialect Cohen would tell about a woman who went into the corner grocery store. "How much a pound for the lamb chops?" she'd ask. The butcher said, "$1.45 a pound." She'd say, "$1.45 a pound? Across the street I can get lamb chops for $1.20 a pound." The butcher says, "So why don't you buy them across the street?" She says, "They're all out of lamb chops." He says, "When I'm all out, they're only 98 cents a pound."

Cohen would tell his story well, but with no frills. The joke stood or fell on its own merits. Flip Wilson would tell jokes, but he would add to them. A little story like the one I just quoted might become a 10-minute routine for Flip Wilson.

Bill Cosby never tells a story in his nightclub routine. He rarely does a one-liner. He makes observations that we all recognize as true—and funny.

There are as many different styles of humor as there are humorists. There can be as many different styles of humor in business as there are business speakers. Don't limit yourself to jokes or stories. If the professionals did that, you might never have heard of Bob Hope or Bill Cosby. You certainly never would have heard of Marcel Marceau.

It may be heretical for me, a comedy writer, to say this, but comedy is not material. It's not jokes, stories, business—none of these. These may be a part of the humor, but the real key to being funny is characterization. It's the attitude.

Let me redeem myself with my fellow writers by elaborating on this point. Most of the comedy writing that I do lately is for Bob Hope. Forgive my ego, but I write very well for Hope. I've been doing it for almost two decades now, so I must be doing something right.

I also speak to businesses, associations, clubs, and just about anyone who will hire a speaker. My talk is humorous, but I can't borrow any of the material that I do for Mr. Hope. Why? It's not a legal or ethical question of borrowing back material that I've already sold. No, I mean that most of the material is written expressly for Bob Hope. It's designed for his style of delivery and his form of comedy. It doesn't work for me.

But isn't funny material funny material? Not necessarily. I've written comedy material for almost 30 years, and I've never written anything funny. It's not funny until it's put into context or until someone breathes life into it.

The stage directions, "She makes a funny face," aren't amusing until Carol Burnett looks at Harvey Korman and raises one eyebrow. The audience now laughs. It's now funny. Then Carol takes that as a cue to change the expression. The audience laughs louder. Now Carol abandons the funny face for just a second and throws Harvey another look. Now the audience is hysterical, and the words, "She makes a funny face," have described something hilarious.

All professional comedians have a unique style that they've developed and the material must fit them exactly. Good, solid, well-crafted comedy material means nothing unless it complements that unique style. That's why my colleagues and I can write material that earns Bob Hope giant laughs, yet won't get any raves for an aspiring young comedian. Why? Because he or she hasn't yet found that comedic voice. We, as writers, don't yet know who we're writing for. We know what Bob Hope is expected to say. We know how Johnny Carson might comment on a particular topic. We feel we can put words into Phyllis Diller's mouth. But we don't know this young comic. Neither does the audience. For us to offer funny words, he or she must develop a funny style.

Let me take this one step further with a hypothetical example. Let's suppose that I'm treating all of my readers to a night on the town. Hypothetical or not, let's limit ourselves to a two drink maximum. We're going out to see two comedians, let's say, Robin Williams and

Bill Cosby. Now both of these gentlemen are polished performers. Each one has exceptional comedy material.

However, before we begin our jaunt, I'm going to take Robin Williams' script and deliver it to Bill Cosby. I want him to perform Robin's stuff tonight. And I'll give Cosby's material to Williams. Do you expect to see two virtuoso performances this evening? No. Why not? The performers are still superior. The material is unchanged. Why doesn't it work?

The comedians are not themselves. They're not working with their own characterizations. They're dealing with a totally different style. They're just not going to be funny.

What does all this philosophical discussion about the comedy styles of professional entertainers have to do with the business speaker? Two things:

1) You need to develop a distinctive, yet natural style of humor. More correctly, you need to rediscover the style you already have, and use that rather than someone else's style.

2) You need to select your material carefully so that it complements your style.

Let's talk about the first point. You've never thought much about a style of humor. You're not interested in a distinctive comedy persona. You're a business person; not a fledgling comic. Why do you have to concern yourself with this style?

Actually, this is more important for your work than it is for the professionals. They do comedy for comedy's sake. If they get laughs, they're successful. You may get giant laughs from your audience, yet be a flop as a communicator. A touch of humor is simply a device to transmit your message. That's all it should be.

A professional comic can be zany, bizarre, wacky. Your humor has to be natural, organic. It must flow from your personality. Anything less might diminish your professionalism.

Let's take another look at professional performers. Some comedians have tremendous staying power. Others arrive, shine brilliantly, and disappear. Why do some, like George Burns, remain popular for a lifetime while others, like Vaughan Meader (the guy who used to do the John Kennedy impression), fade from the show business scene?

I have a theory: the comics who last are the ones that you would like to take home to dinner with your family. That's the test I apply to young comics to see if they have a chance of a long professional life.

What I'm really checking out is whether their humor appears natural. You can imagine how pleasant it would be to have George Burns at your dinner table. First of all, he's a celebrity. That's always exciting, to be rubbing elbows with the great. Secondly, George is fun. He's witty, he's bright. He'd be a delight to talk with. Vaughan Meader was a celebrity, too. He'd be someone special to invite to a family dinner, but if all he did was talk in the John Kennedy voice, you'd grow weary. You'd ask an interesting question and get a Kennedy-like response. Eventually, you'd have to say, "Mr. Meader, be yourself. It's all right. We'd like to get to know you."

I don't mean to imply that Vaughan Meader wouldn't be an interesting dinner guest. What I do mean is that his comedy style wouldn't be. When there is constant tension between the real person and the stage persona, we become uncomfortable. That's why I feel those performers will eventually disappear from the scene, while the more natural ones will continue.

Let me explain one other thing, too. The professional stage comedy of these "natural" comedians is well prepared. It's written with devotion and rehearsed diligently. It doesn't just happen. But the style *appears* natural—that's the secret. I was tempted in that last sentence to say "relaxed." But that would be wrong because "natural" doesn't always mean "relaxed." George Burns is certainly relaxed, but Woody Allen is a funny, nervous wreck. But that's natural because that's Woody. Woody Allen is uptight, so his comedy should be.

Any style that is affected is wrong for you, the business speaker. It may be funny; it may be hilarious. That's great for you as a comedian, but it's not desirable for you as a communicator.

People want to feel comfortable with you at the podium. They want to like and trust you. If your wit is too different from your own personality, it causes a tension, maybe a distrust.

You need to be yourself. We know how much we respect that in candidates that we interview for employment. If they're honest, sincere, and candid, we tend to accept a few of their flaws. If they're pretending to be something that they're obviously not, we wonder what's wrong with that personality they're hiding from us. Audiences, too, wonder about you when you're not totally honest with them—even in doing humor.

Do you enjoy telling stories when you're out with friends or family? Then tell them to your co-workers, your clients, your employees—whoever your audience is. Do it naturally and they'll buy it from you. If you don't enjoy stories or don't tell them well, don't put them in your speech.

Do you use street lingo normally? Then use it in your comedy. If you converse in one-syllable words on the job, don't use four-syllable words in your story telling.

I remember once when a sports writer did a story about a high-school basketball player from our neighborhood. The writer attributed a very controversial statement to the youngster. I asked another friend who played on the same basketball team if this kid really meant what he said. My friend said, "He don't know if he meant it or not. Three of the words in the statement he don't know the meaning of."

Do you speak with literary jargon naturally? Then use it in your wit. W.C. Fields was a comic who loved the multi-syllabic. From him, these stilted sentences sounded typical:

> "I always keep a supply of stimulant handy in case I see a snake, which I also keep handy."

> "What contemptible scoundrel stole the cork from my lunch?"

Notice, it's not "whiskey" or "booze;" it's "stimulant." That's funnier from W.C. Fields, for some reason. He also would call a thief a "contemptible scoundrel" instead of a "jerk."

A good example of different styles, especially in the use of words, was Bob Hope and Bing Crosby in the road pictures. Crosby was an admitted word-lover. He played them the way a jazz artist plays his instrument. I've heard Crosby ask not for a drink but for "a bit of the bubbly." Hope would go for the simple word that made the joke crystal clear, while Crosby would go for the melodic, grandiloquent term that he could almost sing rather than speak. Both were funny, but each was different.

The best style to develop is the one you already have. Capitalize on your own personality because it's the one that requires the least work. It's also the one you've been doing the longest and the one your acquaintances know best. Also it reflects your preferences.

Study yourself and honestly assess your personality. Don't say you don't have one, because even that is a distinctive style. I emceed a retirement banquet for a fellow worker who was a quiet, lackluster gentleman. He wasn't happy with his forced retirement at age 65. We all got nervous when he began his farewell speech at his party because we feared it might be a lament that would kill the festivities.

He said, "What can I do now that I'm leaving my place of employment? Where can I be wanted now that I'm no longer wanted here?" "Oh, boy, this is going to be real fun," we all thought. He went right on. "When racehorses can no longer run, they're retired to stud." His eyes brightened up with that and he said, "Hey! Now there's an idea."

It got laughter and applause.

Now let's talk about the second point, the selection of material. Once a speaker or a performer discovers that comedy voice, it dictates the material that person should use.

As I mentioned earlier, it's easier for a writer to write for Bob Hope or Johnny Carson than for an unknown, though promising, comedian. All of us know what Hope or Carson might say, so we writers compose something that is consistent with that. None of us knows yet what the unknown might say, so it's harder to focus the writing.

There was a great joke in radio years ago. Jack Benny, the quintessential cheapskate, was accosted by a mugger. "Your money or your life," the crook threatened. There was no reply. After a beat, the audience broke into loud laughter. Only Jack Benny would have to ponder that.

The hood repeated his threat, "Your money or your life." Jack Benny said, "I'm thinking it over." The audience roared.

It was the perfect gag for Jack Benny. If Bob Hope's character was asked, "Your money or your life," he might have replied, "I take it you're from the IRS."

"Your money or your life" posed to Johnny Carson might have gotten the reply: "Haven't I been married to you?"

Even comics who are very similar in style have material that is individualized. A writer friend of mine recently had a newspaper article written about her career. The piece listed several one-liners that she had written for various clients. She asked me what I thought after reading it. "I enjoyed it," I said, "but I think the jokes you did for Phyllis Diller should have been sent to Joan Rivers and vice versa." She said, "That's where I did send them. The reporter mixed them up in the story."

When you select or write your material, first consider the form of the humor. Should you use anecdotes, one-liners, simple asides, or quotes from other people? Or should you use all of these in some combination?

You use only those that complement your characterization—your comedy persona. Actually, I shouldn't call it your comedy persona; I should call it your speaking persona. Your material should complement your professional speaking technique.

Decide what you are going to do based on your ability. Can you tell a story? Then tell one. Can you deliver a good one-liner? Then do it. If you can't; don't.

Part of the form, also, is the language you use. Is it literary, conversational, or street lingo? Use whatever gets the point across, provided you're comfortable with it.

When I visit comedy clubs around the country I hear some good material laced with obscenities. Often the vulgar language is not part of the joke; it's there only for emphasis or color. I'm not comfortable speaking in public that way, so I would change that material. If cleaning it up destroyed the comedy, I wouldn't use that humor.

However, I sometimes throw a "hell" or "damn" into my presentation for the same reason. In my opinion, it gives the joke more impact. Some people aren't comfortable with these invectives. Then they shouldn't use them.

The material you select must represent you—your talents, your style, and your beliefs.

You also have to judge the content of your material. You must know what it says and be certain that it says what you want to say. Many well-known comics have been criticized for controversial comments. Afterwards, some of them said, "I had no idea the joke meant that." They didn't mean to offend, they just didn't realize what they were saying. They knew, of course, that the joke was funny, but they didn't look beyond that. As a business communicator, you'd better look.

Also, make sure the humor you're using makes the point you're trying to make. Remember, you're trying to get a message across. You're trying to convey that message more effectively with a touch of humor. You defeat your purpose if the humor conveys the wrong idea.

We've used Abraham Lincoln as our model raconteur. If the accounts in the books are right, he was. His stories illustrate his points very clearly. They are not all hilarious, but they are all enlightening. That's what he wanted. Presumably, it's what all business speakers want.

However, not every one of us has to have the collection of anecdotes that Lincoln amassed. Nor do we have to have a book of jokes always open on our desk. There are as many different styles of humor as there are humorous speakers. With some experimentation and analysis, you'll find the one that works for you. If you're happy with it, the audience usually will be, too.

CHAPTER SEVEN

But I'm Not a Funny Person

Some people complain not only that they can't tell a joke, but that they're not funny. That I don't believe. Everyone can get laughs. Test me. Next time you go to the airport, observe. Eighty percent of the people are fun to watch. They bring chuckles without even trying. That's in the general corridors of any terminal. Go into the VIP rooms, and the percentage rises to ninety percent. How hilarious could those people be if they worked at it?

Don't tell me you've never gotten laughs. I travel around the country and try to be funny at banquets and seminars. Some of my biggest laugh getters, though, have been on the planes travelling to make my speeches. One time I tried to coax some recalcitrant salad dressing out of its tiny plastic container. I coaxed it so well that it blew up in my face. The flight attendants were very attentive and helpful. They also worked quickly: they wanted to get out of my sight so they could laugh their silly heads off.

I avoided this problem on my next flight by upgrading to first class where the salad dressing is served in civilized containers. So are the drinks. I ordered gin on the rocks, which they presented to me in a comfortable, heavy, real-glass glass. I enjoyed one sip and then dropped glass and contents square on my crotch. Pain struck my consciousness first, followed closely by unbearable chills. Embarrassment chased both of these when I realized that I needed assistance—quick. If you want to see how easily you can get laughs try walking down the interminable, narrow aisle of a stretch DC-9—from seat 1C to the service station at the end of the plane—with a wet stain decorating the front of your trousers.

You know you can confess to equally awkward blunders that produced chuckles—maybe not to your face, but behind your back or hidden behind the open pages of magazines. People have laughed at you somewhere. The trick now is to get them to do it on purpose.

I can hear you arguing with this logic in your head. "Sure, everybody does something dumb in their life. We all look stupid from time to time. That's different from getting laughs from the platform." Sure it is, but my point is that you can't classify yourself as a person who can't get laughs. You can, you have, and you will.

As an experiment when I lectured before a regional meeting of Toastmasters International, I asked for volunteers—people sitting in the audience who felt they couldn't get laughs. Many hands shot up. I invited a few of them to come on stage to see if they could get laughs with my help. Three timidly agreed.

I didn't plant these volunteers, nor did I prepare anything with them ahead of time. I had never met them before (I hadn't even known if I would be able to get anyone to volunteer that night).

I had prepared material. I gave each volunteer a copy of his or her script and asked them to study it for a few minutes as I continued with the lecture. Later, they came back onstage to read the dialogue.

One of the volunteers, a soft-spoken woman, took over the lectern and the microphone at my invitation. She was to read a joke that I had guaranteed would produce laughter. She read only a few sentences when I interrupted with some pointers. Her stance wasn't powerful enough. She straightened up and I stepped aside, as she continued. I stopped her again to recommend that she speak with more conviction. She nodded obediently, and went on. I interrupted once more to suggest more effective line readings for her. She nodded approval and continued again. Once more I stepped forward. She quickly turned to me and said, "Will you leave me the hell alone?"

The audience screamed. They loved it. She had stood up to authority. She put this pompous, interrupting ass in his place. What the audience might or might not have known—it really didn't matter—was that her outburst was written into the script. The joke she was reading was irrelevant. It was the set up for this—her put down of me—that was the joke.

The woman who swore she couldn't be funny got big laughs. What's interesting, though, is that the woman enjoyed her new-found skill. Throughout the rest of the lecture, whenever I called on her or she came onstage, she played that same character—the performer who had put the coach in his place.

Each of the other two experiments worked as well. It wasn't that these people couldn't get laughs; it was that they believed in their unfunniness so firmly, that they never tried. They surrendered before the battle began.

An interesting event in my life puzzled me then and puzzles me now. I stood in line to see Phyllis Diller appear on *The Mike Douglas Show* when it was broadcast from Philadelphia. Phyllis asked me to see the performance and then meet with her in the dressing room afterward.

As my wife and I waited in line outside the studio, a young fellow came up to me and said, "Are you Gene Perret?" I said I was. He said, "Come on up to Miss Diller's dressing room. Phyllis has to leave immediately after the show, so she would like to meet with you now."

I met briefly with Phyllis and then went down to sit in the audience for the telecast. As we walked back to the studio I asked the young fellow what made him come right over to me in line. We had never met before. He hesitated to answer for fear that I might get angry. I assured him I wouldn't, and he said, "Phyllis Diller told me to go to the line and find the guy who looked the least like a comedy writer." He picked me first.

Phyllis was doing a joke and his selecting me was coincidence, I'm sure. (At least, I hope I'm sure.)

What does a comedy writer look like? Dick Cavett doesn't look much like Woody Allen, but they're both comedy writers. Some of my colleagues look like fallen-away football players, others like accountants. A few look like international terrorists. We don't fit into a mold that you can classify as "comedy writer."

You can't judge a book by its cover; you can't predict how funny a person will be by their looks. Some, admittedly, you might look at and say, "I hope that person is a comedian because he's never going to make it as anything else." Nevertheless, appearance doesn't determine funniness. Bob Newhart looks as normal as any one of us, but he's funny. Jerry Lewis doesn't look too normal, but he's funny.

Personality, dress, manner of speech, voice volume, facial expressions, gestures—none of these makes you funny. Neither do they rule out your being funny. Look at some of the professional comedians.

Bob Hope and Johnny Carson have a quiet, dignified wit; Buddy Hackett has a boisterous, Brooklyn kind of comedy. Alan King screams his jokes at the audience; George Burns has an unassuming, almost reluctant, humor. Comics can be loud, like Jackie Gleason; they can be timid, like Jackie Gleason's "poor soul." Funny people can be sloppy, careless, and carefree like Oscar Madison in *The Odd Couple*; they can be finicky, straightlaced, and meticulous like Felix Unger.

Humorists can speak out of the side of their mouth, like Buddy Hackett. They can speak with a heavy dialect, like Jackie Mason. They can have a resonant, disc-jockey voice like Dick Cavett. They can whine, like Roseanne Barr. They can stutter. We have a writer on the Bob Hope team who makes jokes of his stuttering. He told me once to give him a call at home. He said, "I-I-If n-no one answers, d-d-don't hang up. Th-th-that's me."

Comics can be strong and athletic, like Bob Uecker, or they can even be physically handicapped. A very good writer in Hollywood who has muscular dystrophy began his career as a nightclub performer. He kidded his handicap. He would say, "I can drive a car, you know, but it's difficult. My automobile insurance costs me $2,400 a year—and that's just on the inside."

Any person or personality can channel humor. You can. I know you can.

Humor accepts all applicants. You can't escape because of size, personality, speech patterns, shyness, or a note from your mother saying, "Please excuse Martha from Wit 101 since she is not funny."

Can a big man get laughs? Brad Gilbert, who won the humor competition on *Star Search* is 6'9". Yet Mickey Rooney gets his share of laughs at only 5'2". Oliver Hardy proved that fat men get laughs; Stan Laurel showed that slender men do, too. Phyllis Diller kids her unattractiveness, but Lucille Ball was a showgirl who did all right with comedy. Good-looking men like Johnny Carson can be funny, and the late Marty Feldman got laughs with his unique face.

The list could run for 26 pages if we allowed it. We could give examples of all different sizes, shapes, and personalities. Regardless of what you look like, sound like, or smell like, you can be funny.

The advantage of all this is that you don't have to change anything to add humor to your talk. You needn't become louder, or more animated in your gestures. You don't have to become more outgoing or more belligerent. The way you are right now is perfect. Be yourself, because there is a comedy style to fit you.

Too often we try to be funny with someone else's style or material. You might be doing a Robin Williams routine when you're more like a Bob Newhart personality. You might be trying to be George Burns when you're really closer to Don Rickles. That's pointless. As some wit once said, "It's like trying to teach a pig to sing. It not only wastes your time, but it annoys the hell out of the pig."

You already have a manner, style, and personality that is tailor-made for you—and for your comedy. You may feel it's not right for comedy because it's not like any humor you've seen. That may be true because no one is exactly like you.

The faults that you feel are interfering with your humor are the ones that might trigger your biggest response. Don't try to hide them behind a Borscht Belt comic's demeanor. Let them shine. Let them be funny.

Remember we discussed earlier that humor is truth. If you want to find the humor in any topic, seek it in reality. That same principle holds for developing your comedic personality.

Each of us is a different person. Each of us is composed of strengths and frailties, pluses and minuses. Be honest about your failings. If you're shy, let your audience know that you know you're shy. If you're a "loudmouth," tell the audience that no one knows that better than you. Audiences are sympathetic and understanding. They normally don't hold our minuses against us, provided we own up to them.

How many times have we heard in national scandals that so and so could have been forgiven if only he or she would have admitted the transgression? "Confess your wrongdoing," Joe Q. Public says, "and I can forgive and forget."

Audiences are not only kind to speakers who own up to their shortcomings, but they're appreciative. Each listener knows he or she has weaknesses. They'd like the speaker to be one of them—to admit to failings of his or her own.

In the opening of my banquet speech I tell about my kindergarten-age daughter who asked me to help her with a poem she had to recite at school. I said, "Sure, Honey, Daddy will help you; but you know that Daddy writes for some pretty famous people. Why don't you let me write something extra special, just for you. Then when you give that at school it'll be funny, it'll be different, and it'll be totally yours." She thought about that for a little while; then she said, "Well, Dad, this is going to be in front of the whole school. I'd rather it be good." The story works well because the listeners enjoy a comedy writer putting down his own comedy writing, instead of boasting about it (which most of us do pretty well, too).

Kidding yourself is not a sign of weakness; it's a sign of a strong self-image—that's a plus for an executive. It's telling your listeners that you have so much confidence in your abilities that you can allow them to take a little ribbing, even from yourself.

Here are a few different ways I've heard professional and amateur speakers kid themselves and their weaknesses:

> I spoke at an awards banquet where a former member of the host association returned for a visit. He was 90 years old. He knew they were going to invite him to say a few words, so he rehearsed a little routine with me before the banquet. I agreed, and here's how we presented the joke to the members.
>
> As emcee, I spoke with this gentleman when he came to the microphone. I asked him how he was doing and he said he was doing just fine. "In fact," he continued, "I just got this new hearing aid which is fantastic. It's expensive, it's state of the art, and it's the best hearing aid money can buy." I took my cue and asked, "What kind is it?" He glanced at his watch and said, "It's about eleven-thirty."
>
> Bob Hope kids his age with, "People ask if you can still enjoy sex over 70. Certainly you can, but it's safer to pull over to the side of the road."
>
> And, "I enjoy sex as much at this age as I ever did—especially the one in spring."

One Toastmaster admitted to being nervous about having to deliver his first humorous talk. He also kidded himself about being short. He said, "I was so nervous about giving this humorous talk that I hardly slept at all. I was up the entire night pacing back and forth under my bed. . . ."

Another speaker at this same Toastmaster meeting kidded his less-than-dynamic personality. He said, "I told my wife that I was worried about this humorous presentation. I said, 'I can't figure out anything to talk about that will get laughs.' She said, 'Just tell them about our honeymoon.'"

Another woman speaker at that affair confessed to her frustration over the humorous speech. She said, "I asked my husband, 'What can I possibly do to get laughs?' He said, 'Enter a beauty contest.'"

Roseanne Barr chides her own performance as a housewife and mother. She says, "When my husband comes home, if the kids are alive, I figure I've done my job."

Phyllis Diller never professed to be a great housewife or cook. She tells about the time "a grease fire broke out in my sink. The firemen arrived and put it out, but three of them had to be treated for food inhalation."

Are you shy? You can't be any more timid than the henpecked husband who said he was "afraid to tell my pregnant wife that I'm sterile."

Some of you may say, "Wait a minute. I don't want to wave my failings before a strange crowd to have them ridiculed." Then don't. That's your decision. Hide them. Cover them. Mask them with make-up. Lie about them, if you want. Don't use them, though, as an excuse to avoid humor.

Humor is very flexible. You can use it to present your idiosyncrasies to an audience, or you can use it to hide those same idiosyncrasies from them. You can use humor as the cathartic that presents your minuses to your audience and begs their indulgence. Or it can be the distraction that camouflages your weakness. It can be a diversion that allows you to escape from an audience with your dignity intact.

If you seriously want to mask a trait, simply manufacture another one and toss it to your listeners. Create something you're not so sensitive about and kid yourself about that. Your audience will bite.

Does any humorist mention anything about Dolly Parton except the obvious? Does Bob Hope razz Gerald Ford about anything except his treacherous golf game? Dean Martin jokes exist today because Dean needed something to build his act around after he split from Jerry Lewis. He decided to become a drunk—a stage drunk.

If you don't want people to kid you about being short, then joke about the way you dress. People will accept it.

I used to write countless flat-chested jokes about Phyllis Diller. "I buy two kinds of bras—plain and mercurochrome," "I put my bra on backwards one day, and it fit," "I have trouble buying brassieres. I take a 32-long." Audiences listen to Phyllis and laugh at these gags even while they're looking at her on stage. She's a well-developed woman.

Probably the greatest example of a mythical defect was Jack Benny as a miser. He was known as the stingiest man in the world because he had his writers, from radio days, paint him that way. He did the jokes on himself, too. He once appeared at a charity golf tournament. After entertaining the gallery at the first tee, the tournament executives insisted that Jack begin play. He turned to his caddy and said, "Are you any good at finding lost golf balls?" The kid said, "Yes, Mr. Benny, I am." Jack said, "Well, find me one and let's get started."

You are you. That's where your humor should begin. Don't bend yourself to fit any material. Bend all material to fit you. Find material, alter material, or write new material that suits you—your personality and your style. You're more important than any piece of material.

As a professional writer, the first thing I have to know with any assignment is who I'm writing for. I have to watch the client perform. I have to see and hear the comedian. That's the only way I can write material that is going to suit that person.

"Suit" may be the proper word because it's like going to a custom tailor. The tailor can't produce a suit until he or she measures you. Likewise, all comedy should be custom-made.

You have a unique managerial style. As an executive you're one of a kind. You follow general precepts, but you follow them your way. You have an individual communication style, too. All of this—

everything that makes you "you"—goes into building your peculiar style of humor.

Begin building your humor from within so that it complements your unique individuality. Don't abandon who and what you are to be a humorous somebody else. Be yourself and enjoy it!

PART II
Delivering Your Humor

"Seriousness is the only refuge of the shallow."
Oscar Wilde

CHAPTER EIGHT

Tips on Delivering Humor

Frustration dreams are common. Pilots dream of trying to take off from a runway that is littered with debris. Dancers dream that their legs become so heavy they can't lift them. A drummer dreams that when he hits the skin of the drum, it shatters. Perhaps these should rightly be called nightmares.

A speaker once told me of a frustrating dream she had. She arrived at the auditorium on the evening of her presentation, was introduced, walked onstage to whatever the singular of applause is, glanced into the auditorium, and saw that only one person was present. Speakers, even in their dreams, subscribe to the "show must go on" philosophy, so she began with her powerful opening. It didn't work. Not because the audience was so small, but because the audience—that one guy—wasn't paying any attention. He was reading something of his own.

After a few minutes speaking into a vacuum, the lecturer finally surrendered. "Look," she said to her audience, "this is a waste of my time and your time. Why don't we just call it a washout and both go back to our rooms?" The gentleman glanced up from his notes and said, "No, I'd rather you continue."

She did. You see, even in dreams, speakers know they don't get their fee unless they perform the service.

As it became more fruitless and more painful, she pleaded again with her listener. "Please continue," he insisted.

She endured through the entire speech, then said sarcastically, "I'm sure there are no questions." There were. The lone listener raised his hand continually, asking inane questions, which she graciously answered. He listened to none of her answers.

The frustration got to her, though. She shouted, "Why? Why do you force me to go on when you don't care what I'm saying. You're not even listening. Why must I continue?" The man said, "Because I'm the next speaker."

I don't believe she ever had that dream. You may not believe she ever told me that story. You're learning too many of my tricks from this book. The story, even if fabricated, makes a point, though. What is a speaker without an audience? It's like the sound of one hand clapping. No, better yet, it's like the proverbial tree that falls in the forest. It definitely makes noise, but no one is there to hear it.

Speaking is communication. It's an exchange of information; exchange is the key word. Someone offers and someone accepts. A speaker requires a listener, as we saw in the opening story—preferably more then one listener.

Humor is a specialized form of communication. It requires the humorist and someone to react to the humor. Audience reaction— whether belly laughs, chuckles, snickers, or smiles mixed with tears— is not spontaneous. That reaction must be orchestrated.

I once had a teacher—not a very inspiring instructor—who told the class flatly, "I don't care whether you learn this stuff or not."

He was right. It didn't affect his life. He offered information to us, told us what we should do to learn it, then withdrew from the process. The rest was up to us. If we learned it, we gained; he neither gained nor lost. If we ignored it, we lost; he neither gained nor lost. He was completely disinterested.

You can be that kind of speaker, if you like. You can prepare your discourse well, present it clearly, and then fold up your notes and leave the podium. Each listener is free to take notes, analyze them, study them, and gain what they want from your lecture.

Speakers can be like that; humorists can't. (And, for those parts of your speech where you present humor, you are, in effect, a humorist.) Humor demands a return from the audience. Without laughter—or an appropriate response of some kind—a humorist is one hand clapping. You can't be dispassionate.

If that teacher I told you about had been paid according to the grades of his students, he would have been very concerned about our learning. He would have forced homework and study on us because he would have had something to gain or lose. In presenting humor, you will always have a stake in how your audience receives it. Not a financial interest; an emotional one. If you're going to do a joke, you want to get a laugh.

If you want something from your audience, you must give to your audience. You can't expect to get laughs; you must earn laughs.

Till now in this book you've been "getting ready" to present humor. You've gathered material, analyzed it, rewritten it. Eventually, you have to face the mike. Some speaker introductions seem endless, but they're not. They do end. When they end with your name you have to stand up and speak.

But not yet—at least, not yet as far as this book is concerned. You still have some preparatory work to do. You need to polish your delivery.

Sometimes an outstanding performer can salvage mediocre material. A bad performance, though, can destroy even the most superb writing. You've worked hard at assembling your humorous material. Since you're the performer, you owe it to you—the author—to be excellent.

These tips should help:

Know you can perform the material: I've worked with many talented, legendary performers—Bob Hope, Carol Burnett, Phyllis Diller, Sammy Davis, and others. They're all limited. Everyone is. Don't misunderstand (and I hope they don't)—their talent is stupendous. They do what they do splendidly. But they do what they do.

The reason they are so successful is because they know their limitations. Professionally, they perform only what they know they can do and can do well.

The rest of us aren't always so smart. We attempt things that we think we should be able to do. We should only try what we *know* we can do. Often our minds or our egos are to blame. Someone explained that Bing Crosby's popularity was due to the fact that most people, in the shower, thought they sang like him. In their heads they did, but a tape recorder would have shown them to be wrong. That's our egos deceiving us. Egos tell some of us that we're as inventive as Robin Williams. Getting no laughs from friends at the party doesn't deter us. Ego tells us that we're funny—contrary opinions be damned!

There is some humorous material that we can't or shouldn't do. Like the professionals, we have to learn our limitations.

Suppose, for example, you have a piece of material that demands a Humphrey Bogart impersonation. It's a funny bit, but it must have a Humphrey Bogart sound-alike. You can tell that joke in your mind and be superb. In your own head you sound exactly like Bogie. However, when you try to tell it aloud, you sound like you're doing an impression of Edward G. Robinson, or maybe Woody Allen, perhaps Joan Rivers, or even Lee Iacocca. Whoever you're doing, it ain't Bogart.

Impersonations are a talent unto themselves. There are other jokes that you may not be able to do. I once auditioned actresses for a role in which they had to scream—and scream convincingly. It sounds simple, but many people can't scream at the top of their lungs. They try, but the sound that comes out is half scream and half apology. Try it yourself sometime and see if you're honestly convincing.

I'm one of the non-screamers. I find it difficult doing any stories that are too loud. I feel uncomfortable, and the audience is never convinced. Here's a story I can't tell:

> A man was explaining how he bagged the lion head trophy that is mounted on his wall. He said to a friend, "I was tip-toeing through the thick underbrush. We knew there was game in the area, but we weren't sure exactly where it was, nor how close. Suddenly, the bushes in front of me parted. This huge cat poked his head through and roared— ROOOAAARRRR!!! Unfortunately, I wet my trousers." The friend said, "I don't blame you in the least. I would have, too." The man said, "No, not then. Just now when I went ROOOAAARRRR!!!"

It's a good story and fun to tell, but I can't do it well. To tell that story effectively, you have to roar loudly—loudly enough to convince an audience that you might wet your trousers. When I roar, it's unconvincing. So I don't tell the story.

Dialects, if they're a part of the story, are another area where people think they sound exactly right, but often don't.

How do you know if you can tell a story effectively? Try it. Say it aloud. It does no good to rehearse it in your head, because in our heads we all sound talented. Say it out loud and honestly evaluate the results. If you can tell it, fine; if you can't, replace it.

Rehearse your humor: If you have a story or bit of humor that you can deliver, now you have to learn to deliver it well. You learn that through practice—through rehearsal.

I still remember the first monologue I delivered in public. It was at a party for my supervisor who was retiring. I wrote a 35-joke routine about him, and rehearsed it every night for a month. I practiced that speech so much that once I started the first joke I couldn't stop until I got to the last one. It became like one long sentence.

Still this was my first try at comedy, so I didn't trust myself. I had the speech in my hand as I spoke, and it went well. The audience was receptive. They laughed; my supervisor roared; and I was hooked on comedy.

A friend complimented me afterwards, saying, "Congratulations, that was a great talk. But tell me something. How could you read that paper with your hands shaking so much?"

I probably couldn't have read it. I had the speech memorized from having recited it so often. As I mentioned, once I started that opening joke, the rest of the jokes just fell out. I couldn't have stopped them if I wanted. The point is that even though I was physically trembling (and I was), my voice didn't falter. I didn't "phumpher" any of the words. Why? Because the rehearsal paid off.

Again our minds can trick us. We have a humorous routine that we know very well. We feel safe with it. However, when we get before the crowd, we can lose it. We forget key words, or suddenly find we can't pronounce them. "Good evening" comes out of our lips as "Geebning."

The only protection is rehearsal.

Now It's Time for You to Speak

At last, the introduction is completed and you step to the microphone—to try your humor. As this book advised earlier, jokes aren't the only form of comedy. Your humor can be an attitude, a gesture, a certain voice inflection, a glance—almost anything. However, since everyone will be doing something different, and since most humor involves story or joke-telling, here are a few tips on telling a joke. Most of them also apply to other styles of humor.

1. Understand your humor: Earlier I told you about a mean joke I pulled on one of my high school classmates. I told a meaningless joke to several accomplices who laughed uproariously at it. All of us were in on the deception except the hapless victim, who laughed when we did. Most people would. We laughed so hard at him that he thought the joke must be funny and he laughed harder. He had no idea what the punchline meant, but he was doubled up laughing. The real payoff came later, as we heard our victim retelling the "joke."

Many of us do that. We hear a joke get laughs. We don't quite understand it, but assume it's funny because other people are laughing. You really can't do justice to a story that way. Why? Because you don't know how to tell it. You don't know what to emphasize. You don't know what expressions or voice inflections to use. You don't know what you're talking about.

I sometimes chuckle to myself when I hear television actors reciting technical medical terms. They're trying to act, but they have no idea what they're saying. "I hate to tell you this, Sarah, but your husband's diaphoresis may be symptomatic of ischemial infarction. We won't know until the pylograms are interpreted by the renologists." How can the actor say that as if he means it when he has no idea what it means? (I just wrote it, and I have no idea what it means.)

Good performers find out what it means. They ask the writer, the director, the producer, fellow actors. Chances are none of them know, either. If not, they'll call a medical doctor and have him reduce the medical mumbo-jumbo to understandable laymen's terms. The point is to know what you're saying before you say it.

Once we had a guest on a variety show. In a sketch about a French restaurant, the writers wrote in a few French words as the order. When the guest, who spoke French, read the script, she went into a fit of laughing. She asked permission to ad-lib her order and we naturally allowed it. What the writers had her requesting as a gourmet meal was "All the bread you want and a glass of meat."

Before telling a joke or story, you should first know that it's funny, believe that it's funny, and know why it's funny. That doesn't mean you should be able to sit someone down and do a treatise on the humor of the given story. No. It's difficult to reduce comedy to an analytical explanation. Someone said it's like dissecting a frog. You may learn something, but you kill the creature in the process.

But you should have a feeling for the humor. Not necessarily a feeling that can be verbalized, but an internal knowledge that you enjoyed the story and there is a logical reason why you did.

2. Know the punchline: This part of the book probably should have been printed in red. If there is any one section that will help people use humor effectively and effortlessly, it is this one. *Know and understand your punchline.*

As a young writer, I heard the producer of a variety show give his staff some advice. To me, it was stupid. It was so obvious and basic that I thought it was dumb even to mention it to a group of professional comedy writers. He said, "You've got to tell the audience when to laugh." I laughed at his advice.

Later I learned it was very solid and useful advice. Comedy, especially professional comedy, is supposed to make people laugh. You can't depend on an audience laughing as one without a cue. You have to tell them when to laugh.

I know this is confusing, so let me illustrate. Suppose you have a trained dog act on stage. The trainer calls the dog toward her with enthusiasm and confidence. The dog never moves. That can be funny, but there is no laugh trigger. Does the crowd laugh as soon as the trainer calls the dog? Probably not. They'll just assume that the animal takes some time to respond. Then do they laugh after five seconds? Maybe. How about after ten seconds? They may be bored with the bit by then and not bother to laugh.

Then how do you trigger the reaction? How do you let the audience know when to laugh? The trainer will do that. She'll call the dog and get no response. Some people might laugh there. After a pause the trainer will look sadly to the audience. Aha! Now they know it's a comedy bit. Now they have permission to laugh.

The trainer can then call the dog again, with a comic punchline. "Come on, girl. It's only an hour show, girl." The audience knows to laugh again.

The point is that in the telling of a joke or story, in trying to get a laugh of any kind, you have to know what the laugh is and where the laugh is. Then you provide the leadership. You tell the audience when to laugh.

Remember, humor is like mentally pulling the rug out from under your listeners. You trick them. You lead them to a certain spot on the rug, you make them feel secure there, then you tug on the rug and send them tumbling. That requires timing.

If they know you're going to pull the rug out from under them, they won't get on it. They won't be tricked. Even if they do get on, and you tip your hand too soon, they'll abandon the rug. You'll be left with a handful of carpet and no joke.

The same is true with humor. The punchline is the trick, the gimmick. Everything leads to that. If it doesn't, you destroy the effect.

When you know your punchline and fully understand the effect that punchline will have, you can then channel everything you say and do—gestures, words, inflections—towards that end.

Abbott and Costello used to do a routine in their movies that illustrates what happens when you don't fully understand the punchline.

Bud Abbott said to the comic, Costello, "Have you ever ridden a jackass?" Costello said, "No." Bud Abbott said, "Well, you'd better get onto yourself."

Later Costello tried to use the same joke on one of the heavies in the film. He said, "Have you ever ridden a jackass?" The guy said, "No." Costello turned around and said, "Hop on, I'll give you a ride."

Know where you're going with each bit of humor you use. Understand the joke and know where the laugh is. Keep the laugh in mind throughout the telling. That will guarantee that everything you say and do builds to that punchline.

3. Tell the story economically: Humor has an economic logic to it. Listeners will invest their time if the humor is worth it. Occasionally they'll get a bargain. They don't want to overpay for a punchline, though. Your best bet as the storyteller is to give them good value. As they say in the commercials, "Give them the lowest prices in town."

Each one of your punchlines needs a setup. You can't have humor without a certain amount of "pipe-laying." But keep the setup concise. Get to the point quickly. Certainly, don't cut the build-up so much that you confuse the punchline. You need to figure out what information you must give for the joke to be understood. Give all the necessary details with enthusiasm and energy, but give them efficiently. Deliver the punch and move on. Don't turn a simple anecdote into a shaggy dog tale.

Suppose, though, you have a tale that requires a long setup. Fine. Do it. That's part of the economy of the joke. However, be sure that the story is worth it. Otherwise, you'll get groans instead of laughs.

One way to tell a longer story and keep the audience satisfied is to add some bonuses along the way. Add a few chuckles to the long buildup. This way the listeners don't feel as if they're "paying" for just the punchline. They're also "paying" for the extras.

Some comics take a simple joke and turn it into a routine. Flip Wilson used to do that. He'd tell one story for eight to ten minutes. When comedians do that, they add punchlines along the way. It's only one story, but it's a series of punchlines.

One word of advice: if you have a good story that doesn't seem to be working, the first place to look for improvement is in the length. Shorten it. Tell it more succinctly. If you get it down to its bare minimum and it's still not working, perhaps you should look for a new piece.

4. Tell your story slowly: One drawback to knowing your story well—knowing why it's funny, knowing where the laugh is, and rehearsing it—is that you often get to know your story too well. Each word is set in your own mind. You know the story works and will get laughs so you can't wait to get to the best part—the punchline.

Many humorists tell their best stories so quickly that they're almost unintelligible. They're like doctors writing a prescription. The medical advice is expert, but only a pharmacist can interpret it—maybe.

Of course, the punchline is the reason for telling the story. It's the cue for the audience to laugh. But, it loses much of its effectiveness if folks have to pause and wonder what you said. They might have an idea, but if they have to supply the syllables they didn't quite hear, they're not going to laugh. It's like doing a jigsaw puzzle with a few pieces missing.

It reminds me of the bit Woody Allen devised with the hold-up note in *Take the Money and Run.* He handed a note to the teller who read, "Give me all your money. I have a gub." She asked, "What's a 'gub?'" Allen said, "It should say 'gun.'" She insisted it read, "gub."

What good is a hold-up note that can't be read? What good is a joke that can't be heard? Take your time and let people hear every word of your brilliance.

5. Be aware of your listeners: Which is a good joke and which is bad? Nobody can tell you that except the audience. The writers, the comedians, the professionals, are all only guessing. It may be an educated guess based on experience, but it is a guess. Everyone in the profession has seen a gag work fantastically one evening only to sit there laughless the next. Why did the first audience react while the second didn't? Who knows? Each audience a performer faces seems to say, "You tell the jokes; we'll decide what's funny."

Whether you as a humorist like it or not, the audience becomes a partner in each of your stories—you would prefer they not be silent partners, of course. They are a part of your humor and can't be ignored.

Be aware of your partners, your listeners. We all are, sometimes. "I don't want to tell this story in mixed company." In effect, you're saying that certain people here won't appreciate this joke, therefore I won't tell it. That's commendable (even if the joke may not be).

Respect your audience. Don't give them stories they don't want to hear. For instance, I have a joke about an ugly tie that my children gave me one Father's Day. I tell the audience I wear the tie because I don't want to hurt their feelings, but I usually wear it to candlelit dinners. "For two reasons," I explain. "It's darker, and I hope the damn thing catches fire." It's a harmless gag, but at church functions "damn" becomes "dumb."

Should you tell off-color stories? Ethnic jokes? That's your call, but your audience should have a vote, too. If they don't want them, don't tell them.

How do you know? First, be aware of who your audience is. Hear your humor as they would hear it. Analyze it from their point of view. If you were sitting out there listening, would you be offended?

You can ask, too. Check with someone who should know. "Would this story offend this audience?" "Would you prefer that I changed this word?" Responsible people will be honest with you because they want a good speech from you.

Remember, you're using humor to enhance your message. If your humor offends, it interferes with what you have to say. It's not worth it. If in doubt, drop it.

6. Leave the laughing to your audience: When you do humor, you're performing. You're entertaining. You become an actor. You have to tell your tale full out, with conviction. Say it and mean it.

I remember Carol Burnett giving some advice to a fine dramatic actor who guested on her show. This person was not used to comedy and tended to laugh when he did or said something funny. Carol said, "When you're angry at me, be angry." In other words, the audience has no fun if the performer is having fun when he or she is supposed to be enraged. If the rage is necessary for the humor, then there should be fierceness in the voice, not a chuckle.

In *The Odd Couple*, Walter Matthau chased Jack Lemmon onto the roof of their apartment building and berated him for being an intolerable roommate. After a vicious harangue from Matthau, Lemmon said, "You want me out of the apartment, is that sort of what you mean?" Matthau glared at him and screamed, "No. That's *exactly* what I mean."

It was a brilliantly funny line, but Matthau the actor couldn't share in the fun. He had to be furious when he delivered it. That was the only way the rest of us could enjoy it. Without that wrath, there was no fun.

You have to be the story teller; not the listener. You have to act out the story; not enjoy the humor of it at the same time.

If you tell an angry story, be angry. If you're confused, act confused. Be whatever the story demands. Don't laugh as you set the story up and don't laugh as you do the punchline—unless, of course, that's a part of the telling.

There are exceptions, naturally—there are to everything. But for the most part, act out your playlet and leave the enjoyment of it to the audience.

"Wait a minute," you say, "Some pretty funny people laugh at their own jokes. It doesn't hurt a bit." I agree. I'm not saying that you can't laugh on stage, or enjoy your own humor along with the listeners. However, tell the story first, and then you can realize, along with the audience, how funny it truly was. Laugh as much as you want at that point.

Don't let your laughter, though, destroy the telling of the tale. Don't let your fun interfere with the audience's fun.

7. Let your humor speak for itself: I'm a professional writer-humorist. I would love to have a scathing comeback for those people who say to me, "Say something funny." Apparently, I'm not a clever enough writer-humorist to pen my own witty response to that request. Usually, I say, "Not for free," or "This is my day off."

But it's a demanding challenge to meet: "Say something funny." I don't need that kind of pressure.

You don't have to create that kind of pressure for yourself, either. When your preamble to a story is, "Here's a great joke," you have to deliver a "great joke." You put an unnecessary burden on your punchline.

Your story may be "great," and you may know it's "great." It's always been "great" before, and it will be "great" this time, too. Fine, but let the audience discover that.

Most good tales don't need a preamble. You usually don't have to introduce good stories. Get to them; the audience will pick up the connection of that humor to your message.

If your story absolutely requires an introduction, avoid superlatives. Let the praise come from the listeners in the form of big laughs.

Does all of this guarantee that every joke you tell is going to work? No. Remember, only the audience knows what's funny. You and I are only guessing.

Are some of your jokes going to miss by a little bit? Are some going to get chuckles where you wanted guffaws? Are some of them going to go over like the proverbial lead balloon? Yeah. What do you do then? That's the next chapter.

CHAPTER NINE

How Do I Know the Jokes Will Work?

This is the beginning of my speech when I give a talk near my own neighborhood:

> "Thank you very much. You know, it's nice to work so close to my own hometown. I don't know whether you know it or not, but I can leave this auditorium, hop in my car, and be back inside my own home in less than five minutes. Now that may not mean much to you, but with the talk I give, to me it can be a lifesaver."

That's only a joke. (Most of the time it's a joke, anyway.) It's a joke, though that reflects a real concern of most speakers. That's the question that people ask most when I lecture to business or professional speakers on comedy: "What do you do if the jokes don't work? My usual, cocky response is, "If that ever happens to me, I'll get back to you."

The arrogance of that flippant reply usually gets a laugh, but it does convey the essence of the answer. Proper preparation is the warranty you're searching for against failure. Do everything that you have to do to guarantee that the jokes won't fail, and surprisingly, most of them won't.

As a comedy writer, I'm sometimes annoyed at the analysis, rewriting, and changing required of some of the scripts that we work with. We study each word of the draft. We spend hours improving just one joke. Enough, already. Why must we put that much effort into polishing an acceptable script?

I got my answer when we were preparing a monologue to be done at a command performance celebrating the 25th anniversary of the coronation of Queen Elizabeth. Bob Hope was running through the cue cards backstage at the Palladium. I sat next to him as he was giving the routine one last look-see.

He dropped one line. Before they could remove the cue card, though, I protested. It was my joke. "Bob," I said, "Why are you taking that joke out?"

"It's not funny." He said. "The Queen won't laugh at that."

I answered, "It's a funny joke. The Queen will love it." (Like I know Queen Elizabeth's taste in humor.)

Hope said, "Will she really?"

I said, "Sure."

He took the cue cards, handed them to me, and said, "Then you do it."

He followed the advice I've given often in this book: When in doubt, cut it.

He had worked hard on this monologue, which would be performed before royalty and seen by millions of viewers on international television. He didn't want to have to wonder, "What do I do if the jokes don't work?"

The first step in safeguarding the effectiveness of your humor is to do the preparatory work. Do everything we've talked about in this volume so far. Work on your material with energy and enthusiasm. Put as much work into your comedy relief as you put into the primary message. It's an investment in your message.

Besides, if you're going to do humor, you want to do it well.

Going back to our example from the Palladium in London, can we assume that all of the monologue jokes were fabulous laugh-getters? No. Some were giant laughs; some were fair; some were disappointments. There might even have been a bomb or two in there.

Then what's the point of all the preparation, polishing, and rewriting, if it still can't guarantee the success of each joke?

We have to take a look at the nature of comedy. Johnny Carson kids often about the "peaks and valleys." He usually mentions it when he's in one of the valleys. It's true. A comedy monologue builds to a crescendo of laughter, trails off, then begins building again. You must have high points and low points. Why? Because many jokes suffer in comparison to other jokes.

I once wrote and produced a variety show for Tim Conway. Tim had been cancelled so many times that his personalized license plate read "13 WKS." That represents the 13 weeks he was on the air before the network decided another show might do better in that time slot. My partner and I were determined to make this a funny, interesting variety show that would get Tim Conway renewed.

After the taping of the premier show, we felt we succeeded. It was a good show. Practically everyone happily congratulated us. Then one of the network executives offered his critique: "You know what was wrong with this show? Some parts of it were funnier than others." This was from one of the intellects who would decide whether this show would be renewed for a second 13 weeks.

I said, "That's our fault. We tried to make them all have the same degree of funniness."

There is no way that a series of jokes in a monologue or sketches in a variety show can be equal. Some have to get bigger laughs than others, and they should. If they were all the same, the result would be monotonous. The bigger laughs add excitement; the smaller laughs set up the bigger laughs. It's Carson's proverbial peaks and valleys.

The same applies to some of the humor that you add to your speech. Maybe the section at the beginning works well, but the routine doesn't get the giant laughs you expected later on. Maybe the ending is powerful, but the bit before it is only fair. None of this spells failure.

Judge your humor by the overall effect. Does it enhance your message? Does it get your audience to listen? Does it prompt them to respect you? Does it help them remember what you say?

This is not to say that you should accept the weaker portions and be content with them. No—try to make them better.

We writers once had an assignment to write special lyrics for a song. There were about 11 places in the song for humor—spots where the music stopped and the comic did a few jokes. We had struggled with this material for about two years.

Finally, the performer called and said that he was happy with all of the material except one joke. It just wasn't working. I called the writers together and said, "Let's write the greatest joke in the world. Let's make this guy happy so we can get rid of this thing once and for all." We did. We worked and reworked until we came up with a selection of about five or six terrific gags.

We sent them off and the next day I received a phone call from our client. "Those new jokes you sent me were fantastic," he said. "I put them into the act last night and they got screams." I couldn't wait to call the other writers to give them the good word. Then the comic added, "You know something, though. They're so funny they make the other jokes look bad. Work on them."

You can always improve the weaker material, but don't be too hard on yourself. Don't surrender because some parts of your routine are less effective than others.

Every baseball player would love to get a hit each time at the plate. Would he settle for a hit every third time at bat? Most would be delighted with a .333 average.

And every batter is going to strike out once in a while. Everyone who attempts humor is going to "bomb." It's not that big a deal, if you can keep your average respectable.

Be careful, though. Ball players hit at a .333 average because they work at it. They take batting practice, watch for defects in their swing, and correct them. They step up to the plate looking for a hit every time. If they relax and say, "I'll only try for a hit every third time to the plate," they'll wind up hitting safely in only one out of each nine tries—or less. Instead of batting .333, they're taking a .111 batting average back to the minor leagues.

Go for the big reaction with all your humor. Be determined to score big each time, but not disappointed when you don't.

Why do speakers ask that one question over and over: "What do you do if the jokes don't work?" It's because professional comics, with their high visibility, have frightened us. "I bombed." "I died." "I stank." Those are all graphic, unpleasant verbs that describe failed humor.

We have to remember that comics are usually insecure people. They worry about their careers. They fret over how much they're loved. They exaggerate. Of course, they have more reason to worry than we have. They earn their livelihood and they earn the audience respect they crave through their humor. If they're not funny, they're not making a living.

But, no business speaker has ever been lynched by an audience angered by an anecdote that bombed.

At best, that anecdote can help your message immeasurably. At its worst—when it bombs, dies, or stinks—it does very little harm. It does very little harm, that is, if used sparingly.

Don't overload your presentation with comedy. Remember, a little cayenne pepper can add character and zest to your chili recipe. Dump in the whole container and you may have to serve fire extinguishers instead of finger bowls. You don't want to be a humorist with a message; you want to deliver a message with a touch of humor.

Too much humor increases your risks without paying proportionate dividends. Fail once and the audience is forgiving; fail a few times and they're disappointed; fail a lot and they begin to suspect both message and message bearer.

Nevertheless, even with dedicated preparation, the correct amount of humor, and polished delivery, jokes still fail. That's never fun. What do you do when you "flop?"

It helps to take it in stride. I once watched George Burns taping a television special. He caused some turmoil when he blew a line. The director had to stop the action; the cameras had to reposition; and the actors had to go back a few pages in the script. George remained calm, looked out into the audience and said, "I'm an old man. What do you expect?"

The audience laughed, applauded, and loved him for it.

Tony Randall is another old pro who has fun with his mistakes. He prepares for possible flubs. He often tells the studio audience before taping begins, "They call me 'One-Take Tony.' I've been in the business over 50 years, and I've never made a mistake during a taping. I don't take any credit for it; it's just luck, I suppose." Then if and when he does blow a line, everyone has fun with it and forgives him.

Dean Martin on his televised variety show would often leave mistakes in the tape. It was part of his mystique. The audience loved it because watching his show was like watching "live" television. Anything might happen at any time and if it did, Dean Martin didn't care. He'd let you see it. He had nothing to hide.

On the other hand, Shelley Berman, was at the peak of his career when a televised documentary showed him losing his cool. While he was performing onstage, a backstage telephone rang. The TV cameras showed his fury when he came offstage. He ranted at everyone in sight and pulled the phone out of the wall. He behaved like a maniac and America didn't like it. His career tailed off after that and many feel that telecast was the reason.

The message to you and me is: "Don't fall apart when your humor does." Keep your sense of humor, which means you shouldn't take the incident too seriously. Remember a sense of humor is the ability to see, recognize, and accept the reality of any occurrence. That's what you need to do here—keep the failure of one chunk of comedy in perspective.

The following thoughts may help you do that:

1. The 'tragedy' is usually magnified: That ill-timed phone call disturbed Shelley Berman much more than it did the audience. "It destroyed the entire mood of the piece," he claimed. "It ruined my entire performance." It didn't.

In Mr. Berman's defense, the documentary distorted the actual happening. That backstage phone rang once before, at a less critical part of his act. He joked the interruption away and continued his act. Afterwards he asked the backstage workers to disconnect the phone during his performance. They forgot. Then when it rang a few days later at a critical part of his dramatic finish, he blew his cool. The documentary implied that these incidents happened in reverse order— he blew his stack first and then joked the incident away later.

Regardless, neither incident was that momentous. The audience would have tolerated both interruptions. Mr. Berman, though, abandoned logic and reason when the second one occurred. The reality of the events didn't justify his reaction.

If you can keep your sense of humor and at least postpone any over-reaction, you'll usually find on reflection that the "tragedy" was no tragedy after all.

2. The "tragedy" is more painful to us than it is to our audience: When we tell a bad joke or an anecdote that doesn't work, we're embarrassed. We feel we've made fools of ourselves before an auditorium filled with people. Someone once convinced me that embarrassment is a reverse form of ego. If we have a slight stain on our tie, we think the entire world will notice. We feel we're so important that every stranger we pass on the street will inspect our tie and condemn us for that blotch. If we tell one joke in our speech that doesn't work, we immediately project that this crowd will do nothing else all day except discuss among themselves how badly this one story fared. We are frightened, panicked, terrorized. Our concentration can be affected throughout the remainder of the program.

Chances are that hardly anyone noticed. If they did, the failure wasn't as momentous as we thought. Even if it was, probably no one will take it out of the auditorium. They have more important things scheduled for the rest of their day.

A dumb incident once showed me how little others really notice us. A fellow I was working with agonized over shaving his beard. He was tired of it and it was bothering him. Yet he felt it was a part of his personality, a feature that all of us had grown attached to. Was it fair for him to decide arbitrarily to shave it off?

Well, he did. None of us noticed. We worked with him all morning and never commented on his naked face. (Well, almost naked—he kept the moustache.) We honestly never missed the beard.

When we went to lunch, he confessed that he was offended. He felt like the wife whose husband didn't compliment her new dress.

We lunched at our usual cafe. We had been eating there for over a year. We knew everyone and everyone knew us. As soon as we walked in, we presented our newly shaven friend to our waitress. We said, "Do you notice anything different about Barry?" She didn't. We urged her to look closely. Still nothing. We prompted her to look closely at his face. Now she sparked. Her eyes lit up and she said, "Oh, sure. You've grown a moustache."

People don't analyze us as much as we think they do. They won't analyze your humor as much as it seems when you're on the podium, either.

Any glitches in your routine will be more painful to you than they will be to your listeners.

3. The audience is rooting for you: A speaker and an audience are not adversaries. There may be a touch of the love-hate syndrome, but generally the audience is on the speaker's side. Why shouldn't they be? They have to be there to listen. It makes sense that they would want you to be entertaining.

An occasional disappointment in your presentation won't turn them against you. Falter slightly and they'll rush to your support.

The only way they might abandon you is if you force them into it. Try to blame them for your problems, and you'll polarize them against you. If you blame yourself, though, you'll have a roomful of supporters.

That's why I'm uncomfortable with speakers who focus on the negative—even if they're justified. I've seen lecturers with bad microphones who remind the audience of it every two or three minutes. I've seen performances where a light flickered. The speaker wouldn't allow the audience to ignore it. She kept mentioning it throughout her stay on stage.

This is a strictly parenthetical suggestion, but in a sense it ties in with humor that fails. If anything goes wrong with your presentation, whether it's your fault or the promoter's fault, work through it. You might mention it, and perhaps ad-lib about it, but then forget it. Continual reminders distract from your message and your effectiveness. Anyone should be able to give a speech under ideal conditions. All of us, though, must be able to work under flawed conditions.

In most cases, if you're honest and have a sense of humor, the audience will be supportive.

One friendly warning, though: If you do ad-lib, keep the comedy aimed at yourself. Caustic comments directed towards the audience, the promoters, or anyone else can be offensive. You may run into the same kind of disapproval that Shelley Berman did. It's much safer to make yourself the brunt of your comments.

At a banquet talk I gave, a ceiling light fixture flickered a few times and went out. An ad-lib could have kidded the hotel about not paying its electric bill. I might have kidded the host association about only booking the room till a certain hour. But these could have been misinterpreted. Instead I said, "I've often had people doze off during my talk, but never an entire chandelier."

4. The audience will enjoy your frustration (if you do): Carson nightly turned his "bombs" into "blockbusters" by kidding about them. Some people even feel that he planted one or two "clinkers" into his monologue so that he could joke about them.

The most fun I ever had at a lecture was one time when I could hardly deliver the talk. The room next door featured a piano player and an opera singer. We only heard the highest notes of the performance, but they seemed to come at the most inopportune times. We—the audience and I—enjoyed it. We laughed at the situation together. I laughed so hard that when things finally quieted down, I could hardly speak.

People like those gaffes. That's why the rash of blooper shows we had on TV were so popular. Folks like to be "in" when things go wrong.

Your gaffes may turn into gems if you allow the audience to see them and be a part of them. Have fun with them as Carson does. They may turn out to be not only less painful, but a big plus for your presentation.

So far, though, I'll admit I've only postponed answering the question. I've discussed how a joke that doesn't work isn't tragedy. It might even be a camouflaged blessing. But the question remains: "What do you do when the jokes fail?"

Okay. Here are a few tips:

Forge boldly ahead: Don't let any disturbance disrupt your presentation more than momentarily. No turmoil should completely disrupt your talk. Recognize it, assess it, then proceed as well as you can—even when your bad joke is the "disturbance."

When I first began as an amateur public speaker, long before I became a writer, I hired a sound company to record my routine. I was going to have a hit record like Bob Newhart and Shelley Berman. The engineer placed microphones strategically throughout the audience to record the laughter. He had me miked properly. He did a great job. I didn't.

Everything I did bombed. It was awful, and it was painful. All I wanted to do was get the evening over with, slither off the stage, pay the nice man for his work, and go home for a good cry. First I had a lesson to learn.

The sound engineer chastised me. I thought, "I don't have enough trouble. I just stunk up the auditorium in front of my friends, now the guy in the headset is going to torment me."

I said, "I had a bad night. The jokes just weren't working. What was I supposed to do?"

He said, "You're supposed to work harder. Your first few jokes didn't work, so you quit."

He was right. I abandoned all energy and enthusiasm. I just recited the words. I destroyed any joke that had a chance to work. The audience was trying to make me a success, but I bailed out on them.

You have to keep going with increased passion. When things aren't going right, you need to challenge the listeners—confront them. You have to say in your own mind, "I'm going to give the rest of this performance everything I've got. Right now it's not looking too good, but when it's over, if it hasn't worked, it won't be because I surrendered."

John Wooden, the incredibly successful coach of UCLA's basketball team, claims that he never once mentioned winning to any of his players. He urged them only to do their best. His theory was that giving your best is all you can do. If you're good enough to win, you will. If not, you won't. That's out of your jurisdiction. But you can always give everything you've got.

That's good advice in doing humor, too. Give it a lot of excitement and zeal. If it doesn't work, then there's not much more you can do about it.

Acknowledge the failure: When a joke misfires, admit it. You don't have to humiliate yourself from the podium, but if a gag falls flat, don't be the only one in the hall who doesn't notice it.

Don't get carried away, either. If a piece of humor gets a moderate response, that's not a failure. Remember we advised that not every joke is a giant laugh-getter. Some are just chuckles. No, we're talking about the bombs. The ones that get no response beyond a stare. Those you own up to.

I've heard comics say after a non-joke, "Boy, and I thought that was going to be my biggie."

Bob Hope did a clinker on board ship off the coast of Beirut. He told the cue card guy to "roll that joke up in a big ball and fire it towards the enemy—if we can ever figure out who they are."

Sharing your frustration with the audience gains sympathy. It also invites them to have some fun along with you, and at your expense.

One reason for using humor is to gain the respect of your listeners. This reaffirms it. It convinces the audience that you know how your material is being received and that you're strong enough to deal with it if it's not going as well as you expected.

Prepare some "savers": Tim Conway used to get laughs at rehearsals of *The Carol Burnett Show.* Any time his scripted lines didn't get laughs from the staff and crew, he'd mutter audibly, "Saver, saver, saver."

A saver is a line that salvages an unfunny scripted line. Conway would stockpile them and spring them as adlibs during the taping. That's why Harvey Korman struggled for nine years to keep a straight face when working with Tim.

They're not a bad idea for your presentation, either. You won't need that many because you're not going to have that many humorous pieces misfire. Most of the time your humor is going to crackle. When it doesn't, though, a "saver" filed away in your memory can turn your flop into a fantastic funny.

Don't resort to savers promiscuously. They're not for humor that works moderately well; they're for gags that flop. If you use them too often, the audience is going to get the impression that your material isn't working. That could backfire on you.

Here are a few examples of savers. Each of these follows a joke that has not worked.

> "My wife told me that story would never work. I can see you all side with her."
>
> "I wasn't going to do that joke, then I changed my mind. I can see as I glance around the audience that my first instincts were correct."
>
> "You'll have to forgive me; that's the first time I ever tried that story in public—and the last." (That might earn you applause.)
>
> "That's my favorite joke and nobody ever laughs at it but me. I don't care; I'm going to keep telling it. I have to have some fun up here, too, you know."
>
> "You won't hear that joke ever again—anywhere. I kind of wish you hadn't heard it tonight."
>
> *(If you want to kid somebody that the audience all know.)*
>
> "That's the last time I ever buy a joke from Mr. So-and-So."

8. Be aware of your audience and alter your routine: While you're doing all of the above, also notice what your audience likes and dislikes. Often there is a pattern that you can use to your advantage.

They may like the short jokes, but not sit still for the longer stories. They may not enjoy being kidded about themselves, but laugh at the material about the competition.

Each audience will be different, but you may learn from listening to them when some of your pieces don't get the response you expect.

You've probably heard a nightclub comedian tell a slightly naughty gag (or a downright dirty one), and after the laugh say something like, "Oh, it's that kind of a group, huh?" That comic is probably not kidding. He or she might have tried that gag out just to test the waters. It will determine what the rest of the entertainment will be like.

If the only pattern you notice is that this crowd doesn't enjoy any of your humor, then—"If in doubt, cut it." Cut your comedy and just offer your message.

What do *I* do when the jokes don't work? Well, if that ever happens to me, I'll get back to you. Yes, that's my standard reply and it usually gets a laugh. Why? Because everyone knows that sometime, somewhere, a joke is going to fall flat. It happens to everyone. It happens to me; it happens to Bob Hope; it'll happen to you. It's no big deal.

The big deal is to continue to use humor well and wisely, understanding that once in a while it won't work. Don't fear that. Don't be afraid of your audience. They won't attack when the gags fall short. Go out there and have a little fun with them. If a joke or two doesn't work, have fun with that. The audience is friendly. Be friendly back. Enough of your humor will work. Trust me.

CHAPTER TEN

How Do I Avoid Offending Anyone?

Consider this harmless little ditty that you may have heard in your early elementary school days:

> Roses are red,
>   Violets are blue,
> You look like a monkey
>   And you smell like one too.

I called that harmless, but is it? If you were to use that from the platform or in some publication, you might get notes from any of the following:

An irate florist might chide you for using roses as a weapon of insult. Traditionally, the rose has been a symbol of love and romance. How dare you demean this lovely bud by using it to introduce such a blatantly offensive message?

An infuriated botanist may tell you that violets are not blue. They are the most captivating shades of violet, hence the name. To call them blue is to diminish their allure.

A zoologist might be incensed by your disparaging comments about one of God's most enchanting creatures—the monkey. Don't you realize that their intellect is very close to man? Don't you appreciate the good they've done for humanity, say—in the space program—to name just one? Don't you understand that an animal's odor is part of his survival mechanism, that it serves a purpose in the wild? Those innocent little animals are as clean, if not cleaner, than you are.

In doing humor, should you worry about those pen-pals: the florist, the botanist, and the zoologist? I don't think so. There are those people who are inordinately defensive about anything that concerns them. They have no sense of humor about themselves. Those folks have a problem that is beyond the scope of this book. If we limited our humor because of them, there would be no laughter left in the world.

This doesn't allow us humorists carte blanche to attack anyone with immunity. Often the complaints against us are valid. For instance, not all used car salesmen are thieves; not all mothers-in-law are battle-axes. We should avoid unfounded generalizations, gratuitous accusations.

(In fact, I should apologize to the florists, botanists, and zoologists of the world. I didn't mean to discredit them.)

As a humorist, you have to separate honest protesters from humorless cranks.

There is one person you need to be concerned about in this example, though. That's the guy or gal you're saying it to. You've just told someone that he or she smells like a monkey. Despite what the zoologist contends, that's generally presumed to be an insult.

Now there's "malice aforethought." You've aimed a jest directly at a specific person. You maligned that person's odor. You're guilty.

Does that mean that you can't do humor like this? No, it means that you need to be aware of your audience and aware of the consequences of your comedy.

Humor, as we've seen, can be a powerful communication tool However, like most power it must be handled carefully. It can misfire, backfire, or simply be abused.

Humor can hurt others intentionally. It can be used not as a tool, but as a weapon. I don't advocate that. To me, humor is a valuable asset, and I hate to see it misused.

However, it might be used effectively as a device that doesn't injure, but stings. I remember once when our community had a problem with its roads. Streets were in dangerous disrepair. Community groups went through channels, went around channels, and invented some new channels, but the authorities paid no attention. The streets went unrepaired. Then a local columnist did a satire on our streets in the community paper. It was so scathingly funny that the city fathers finally fixed the potholes. They did it to get that "comedian" off their backs.

That kind of humor might have been a little painful for some, but it was necessary. It was like the prick of a vaccination. Its long term benefits outweighed its short term unpleasantness.

Humor can also hurt others unintentionally. That's what we all want to avoid. Our humor is used to enhance communication, not to wound innocent parties. And, any humor that wounds another, even unintentionally, hurts our presentation. It creates an unnecessary tension that distracts from our message.

Have you ever been a houseguest where your hosts were having a spat? Even if no angry words are exchanged, the silent animosity is upsetting. If the argument is verbal, it's worse. You don't feel comfortable in that situation. You either want them to settle the dispute or you want to leave. That's the way your audience feels when your humor is offensive, even unintentionally.

Your first safeguard against injurious comedy is your attitude. What's in your mind when you create or deliver it? Is it revenge? Spite? Ego? "I'll show them?" All of these are dangerous. Your humor can develop a cutting edge that could put off your listeners.

If your attitude is a spirit of fun, your humor is more secure. It shouldn't hurt. Take, for example, these lines complaining about our income tax system:

> "The new simplified tax forms have only three questions: How much did you make? How much do you have left? How soon can you send it in?"

> "Here's a way the government can really simplify income tax returns. Just print our money with a return address on it."

> "They say you can't get blood from a stone—unless you work for the IRS."

Are these vicious, scathing lines condemning an unfair tariff? I doubt it. They're good-natured, humorous jabs at a necessary evil. As Will Rogers, the beloved American humorist—who did as many jokes about income tax as anyone—said, "America is a great country, but you can't live in it for nothing."

Consider, too, our opening four-line poem, "You look like a monkey, and you smell like one too." Is that an offensive line or some friendly kidding? You can't tell because you don't have enough information. You have to know what was behind it. Was it meant to hurt or was it meant to tease?

The proper attitude in using humor is your first safeguard, but it's not a guarantee. Humor, even when delivered in fun, can sometimes offend. I don't mean the kind of offense that our thin-skinned florist, botanist, and zoologist felt. I mean a real hurt that you regret.

Even Will Rogers, who warned us not to have any malice in our humor, sometimes offended people. In 1926, at a banquet of the Old Trail Drivers Association in San Antonio, Rogers was honored by Mrs. R.R. Russell of the Ladies Auxiliary. She pinned an honorary membership badge on the comedian and sat next to him through the banquet. When Rogers spoke he said, "You Old Trail Drivers . . . did all right. You'd start out down here with nothing, and after stealing our cattle in the Indian Nation, you'd wind up in Abilene with 2,000 head or more."

Mrs. Russell stood up and shouted, "My husband was no cattle thief. Don't insinuate that he was."

Newspaper photos of the event show that Mrs. Russell was not at all pleased with Rogers' after dinner oratory. I don't blame her. I'm a Will Rogers fan, and even though he meant no harm—there was no malice in his heart—this seemed like the wrong gag to use at this banquet.

There are a few ways that humor can be hurtful.

Misinterpretation

As a creative exercise in some of my humor seminars, I have people work with words. We take a basic, simple word—"A common ordinary word, something you might find around the house," as Groucho Marx used to say on *You Bet Your Life*—then we try to find several other meanings for that word.

To show you what I mean, let's use the word "house" as an example. We all feel we know the meaning of that word. We can picture it clearly in our minds. Are you picturing, though, the same thing that I'm picturing when I use the word house? We don't know. We don't have enough information.

With very little effort, I'll bet you can find about seven valid, recognized, everyday uses for the word "house." Try it. Close the book for a few minutes and see how many different uses of the word "house" you can come up with. When you're done, come back and read the ones listed here:

1) a dwelling

2) a gambling casino, as in "house rules," or "the house takes a percentage of the bet."

3) a branch of our government

4) a bordello, as in "a house is not a home."

5) attendance at a theatre, as in "count the house."

6) a family or dynasty, as in the "house of David"

7) to contain, as in "the museum will house the original autobiography of Benjamin Franklin."

There are probably others. You can do this exercise with many common words, including some that might surprise you. The word "butterfly," for example, might have several different meanings. It's the pretty little critter that floats around flowers; it's also what they do to a filet mignon when you ask for it well done; it's also the queasy feeling you get in the pit of your stomach when you're nervous. You could probably uncover a few more.

Why bring that up here, when we're discussing humor that might be offensive? Because it's a potential area of misunderstanding. If you're not careful with your words, listeners can misinterpret them.

I once wrote a parody of Cinderella for a nightclub act. Several notable people of the day were cast as characters in that fairytale. One very well-known politician was the "Fairy Godfather." He was the good guy in the parody. He was a well-liked public figure and I thought making him the hero would be a smart idea.

It wasn't. People got angry at this piece of material because of the negative implications involved in the role. Can you guess why?

Right. The use of the word "Fairy" led many people to think that we were comedically implying that this official was homosexual. That was never intended and nothing else in the parody could have led anyone in the audience to assume that. It was strictly a misreading of one word—yet it was a common word. The woman in the original was called the "Fairy Godmother," so it seemed natural that a man in the parody would be named "Fairy Godfather."

"Godfather" was the other troublesome word. Since 1972 and the award-winning film, "Godfather" connotes a mob leader. Listeners felt that we were implying gang connections by calling this politician a "Godfather," even though nothing else in the script insinuated that.

We had to drop the routine, an otherwise funny one, from the nightclub act. It angered, rather than entertained.

There's another interesting aspect of communication. It's a mind-to-mind intercourse. It sounds simple. You say something and people hear it. But, it's more complicated. In fact, the message goes through at least four steps.

First, it must exist in your mind, the mind of the speaker. You have to know what you're going to say.

Second, you translate your thought to words; and that translation is not always accurate. You may not say what you mean. Words are not ideas; they're just descriptions of ideas. You may not choose or be able to find the words that say exactly what you're thinking. We haven't even gotten past the speaker yet and already we have several areas for misunderstanding.

Third, people have to hear your words. They don't always hear what you say. We always kid about a language we used to use in my hometown of South Philadelphia—it was a language that was peculiar to that part of town. For instance, what is meant by the phrase, "Jeet jet?" It means, "Have you had your dinner?" So when one of my buddies says, "Jeet jet?" that's exactly what people hear, but that's not what he meant. He meant, "Did you eat yet?" It's another chance for error.

Fourth, whatever the people hear—whether it's what we said, or not; whether it's what we meant to say, or not—now must be interpreted in their minds. The words they hear become ideas, and we've already noted that words can only approximate ideas.

So you have to think something and then say what you think you thought—although it might not be the thought you think you thought. You have to say what you're thinking, but you might only be saying what you're saying—and not what you think you're saying— which is what you thought. Someone has to hear what you think you're saying, but it could be what they think you said and not what you thought you said. To them, then, what you think you said is not what they think you said. They think about what you thought you said and think they know what you thought, but they only think they know your thoughts. Get it?

Now if that explanation doesn't prove that the process is ripe for misunderstanding, then you've misunderstood my whole point.

Before being reelected to his second term in office, Ronald Reagan addressed a group of young people at a drug rehabilitation center.

"When you get along to where I am," the 72-year-old President said, "you find out that taking care of that machinery (your body) sure pays off when . . . you can still tie your shoes and pull on your own socks without sitting down—and do a lot of things that are much more enjoyable than that." The President smiled.

The young audience, though, laughed. Why? They thought it was a reference to sex. Reagan later explained that he was talking about riding horses, chopping wood, swimming, and diving.

Regardless of what he meant, the audience heard "sex."

This just proves that you must consider your words carefully in communicating. Since humor often skirts the boundaries of respectability, it's even more important that you convey your meaning exactly.

Review the humor you use. Double check for double entendres. I don't mean the blue material type of double entendre—I mean innocent words that could have a second or third meaning.

I recently spoke to a group of pharmacists. I had to, at their request, be sure that I didn't use the word "drugs." These people are pharmacists and they dispense medicine. "Drugs" in today's culture has a new meaning that they rightfully disassociate themselves from.

In speaking to politicians, the word "fix" may be off limits. You and I "fix" a flat tire; politicians "adjust" a flat tire.

Also, look for hidden meanings in your humor. Can it be misinterpreted? Are you really saying what you mean? Or are you going to be like the man who said, "I'm an atheist. I swear to God I am;" or the radio broadcaster who said, " . . . this movie stars Burt Reynolds and Dolly Parton. Boy, what a pair!"

Beware of Related Issues

Suppose you're the banquet speaker and you want to kid the president of the organization, so you pick some standard, universal topic that applies to almost everyone. You decide to kid him about his marriage.

> "During dinner Charlie and I were talking about marriage. He told me he never knew what true happiness was until he got married—then it was too late."

> "Charlie told me that he and his wife have a perfect 50-50 arrangement. Every time he makes 50, she spends 50."

> "Charlie's wife is with him on this trip. She likes to make the trips with him. Well, wouldn't you? It's easier than kissing him goodbye."

Those feel like fairly harmless gags and you certainly want to deliver them in a spirit of fun. Some kid him, some kid her, so you avoid taking sides. These jokes might get a laugh, but not if everyone in the association knows that Charlie and Mrs. Charlie are in the process of filing for divorce.

Related circumstances can change the nature of your humor.

I manufactured that example. Of course, if you were going to kid with such personal material, you should have checked to make sure it's all right. But, some of the other examples I've seen and heard are too unpleasant to repeat!

I once saw a young comic get booed off the stage in a comedy club when he did a routine about children. A horrible kidnapping had been in that town's newspapers for the past week. His material, which flirted with bad taste to begin with, became grotesque.

It's impossible to think up all the situations that might arise, because there are so many variables, but you should be aware that even the most innocent material can be affected by situations that you may know nothing about.

If you can't know about these things, how can you protect against them? First, be aware of possible dangers. If you're going to tease a man about his marriage, find out about that marriage first. Check with people who know him well.

Second, be aware of potential danger in your own material. Would some of it border on the edge of propriety under normal conditions? If it does, it won't take much to push it over that edge. Question the use of that material. Even if you decide it is acceptable, check with someone who knows the group to make sure you won't offend this particular audience.

Some areas that might be trouble: stories about drinking, traffic accidents, death, physical disabilities. You get the idea. Double check any humor that might be described as "black comedy."

Even perfectly innocent jokes can backfire. I check material in one of two ways when I speak to associations. I very quickly review my presentation with my contact, the program chairman, the association president, or whoever. Not so they can evaluate the effectiveness of it, but so they can warn me of anything that's potentially offensive. Second, at a cocktail party or hospitality suite before my talk, I tell a few of the anecdotes to individuals or small groups. The reaction they get at that level can warn me what to use and what to cut from the presentation.

If your material is tasteful and considerate to begin with, an adverse audience reaction is rare and usually not disastrous. Nevertheless, once aware of the potential dangers, you can take reasonable precautions.

Insult Humor

This has to be offensive, right? After all, it is insult humor. Webster defines "insult" as "gross abuse offered to another either by words or actions; any act or speech meant to hurt the feelings or self-respect of another." That sounds pretty offensive, doesn't it?

Suppose you see two men meeting at an annual convention. They know each other, but they haven't met in a year. They shake hands politely and exchange greetings:

"How are you?"
"Fine. And yourself?"
"Not bad. Did you just get in?"
"Yes. I haven't even checked in yet."
"Well, I'll see you around."
"Yes, I'll be at the party tonight."

And they part.

Now picture two other men who meet at the same convention. They haven't seen each other all year, either.

"Boy, they let anyone into this hotel, don't they?"

"Hey, how are you? You know, you get uglier every time I see you."

"Look who's talking. I love that suit you got. I understand that style is coming back."

"You going to be at the party tonight?"

"Not if you're going to be there, I'm not."

"Let's have a drink later. You're buying."

"I'm sure I am. You haven't picked up a tab since 1976."

And they part.

Don't you agree that the first two guys were probably acquaintances, and the second two were most likely close buddies? Insult humor is an acceptable form of social behavior today. Especially so since the Friars and Dean Martin's television show popularized "the roast."

Insult jokes are acceptable, but they're delicate. I've found them powerful and useful. But they must be handled with care.

Follow these rules:

1. Kid people about what they kid themselves about: When people kid themselves, they're usually giving notice that they're not sensitive about that topic. Sometimes, granted, it is their way of masking how they really feel—only they know that for sure. But it's never safe to assume that you can kid people about anything. Some bald people laugh at their baldness; others won't admit they're bald and don't want you bringing it up. Some companies readily admit that Project X from last year was an unqualified flop; other companies don't want their dirty linen aired at the annual awards banquet.

However, if you attend a few seminars and everyone is joking about Project X, you can assume that one or two tasteful lines at the banquet won't offend anyone.

2. Kid about things that don't matter: Bob Hope has kidded every President who ever was in office. Most of the barbs, though, are inoffensive. Why? Because when you analyze them, they're not really about the issues. They're simply kidding a man in a very visible office about something entirely apart from his job.

For example, Hope kids Gerald Ford constantly about his golf:

> "You never have to count strokes when you play with Jerry Ford. You just look back along the fairway and count the wounded."
>
> "You can always spot Jerry Ford on the golf course. His cart is the one with the red cross painted on top."
>
> "There are over 150 golf courses in the Palm Springs area, and Jerry Ford is never sure which one he's going to play until his second shot."

None of those passes judgment on Ford's tenure as President. They don't dispute any of his policies. They simply kid his golf game. No politician lives or dies on his golf handicap.

A relatively safe topic to select for insult humor is one that's far away from a nerve, one that avoids any real controversy.

3. Kid about things that are so bizarre that no one can take them seriously: If everyone knows you're kidding, the malice disappears from the insult. Everyone—at least every-reasonable-one—should know you're kidding if what you're saying can't possibly be true.

I once did a monologue at a party for my Mom. I kidded her about how she kept my brothers and me so neat and clean when we were young:

> "Mom used to keep my brothers and me so clean that we always thought we were for sale."
>
> "Mom put starch in everything. I sneezed once and cut my nose on a handkerchief."
>
> "Everything we owned had starch in it. My brother fell out of bed one night and broke his pajamas."

No one could think ill of Mom from those gags because no one could believe any of them.

Those rules will help keep your insult humor from being insulting. Be careful, though. Just following them doesn't guarantee that any humor you do will be inoffensive. Your attitude is important, too. If there's malice in your heart, there can be malice in your jokes, even if they adhere to these guidelines. Keep your humor humorous. Insult in a spirit of fun and you'll be safe.

Check out insult material carefully. Get a second opinion from someone who knows. And follow this book's standard edict: "If in doubt, cut it."

CHAPTER ELEVEN

Pitfalls That Take the Fun Out of Humor

I once spoke at a company function and did a whole routine about a duplicating machine in our department. This wasn't a simple little reproducing machine that you see in today's modern offices. This was an ammonia blueprinting machine that reproduced drawings up to six-feet-wide and practically unlimited length. It was a large, expensive contraption that never worked properly.

That's what my jokes were about. I kidded about this being a valuable machine to have in a drafting office; it ate harmful blueprints. I made some management-oriented crack about it working less than someone whose brother-in-law was the shop steward. Gags like that.

I thought they were funny. One gentleman didn't. He was the supervisor of the department that operated and maintained the machine. He was under some pressure from his manager, who surely was under pressure from his vice-president, to get the machine functioning consistently and efficiently. He was hurt and embarrassed by my routine and left the banquet.

The jokes were funny; the evening wasn't fun for me or for him.

The purpose of the humor we've discussed in this book is to enhance your message. It's to get people to listen and remember what you say. It is easier to do that when you amuse, entertain, and refresh your audience.

Humor is not the only device that accomplishes this. In your business communication you may resort to shock value at times. Perhaps threats work on occasion. Offering rewards can get people to listen and act. All of these are valid devices along with many other dramatic ones. They're all beyond the scope of this volume, though. We're discussing humor as a communications tool. It isn't always "belly laugh" comedy. It can produce a chuckle, a smile, a grin, or even just a raised eyebrow and a nod of recognition. But it should be fun.

Anything that interferes with that fun interferes with this message.

There are a few booby traps to be aware of:

1. Humor that's too aggressive: Generally, this is humor that's not designed to entertain or amuse; it's meant to punish. It's not there to enhance a presentation; it's there to gain an unfair advantage in a personal battle.

The example that I used to begin this chapter was an honest misjudgment on my part. I was speaking at a company function to company executives, and I joked about something that mattered. But common sense should have warned me that someone would get hurt.

Suppose, though, that my department had been feuding with this supervisor's department over that duplicating machine. Let's say that my work was being delayed because he refused to take the time or spend the money to fix the machine. Then my jokes would have a new meaning. They would have shown upper management that this gentleman's department was a liability. The laughs from the audience would have indicated that the whole facility knew how ridiculous this outdated piece of machinery was.

It would have worked, too; but it wouldn't have been humor—at least not the productive type of humor we're talking about in this book.

Aggressive humor is like the kids in the schoolyard who quarrel with childish "Oh yeah? Well, your mother wears army boots," type of invectives. The one with the most supporters gets the most derisive laughs, and wins.

Some use this aggressive humor (or aggression disguised as humor) to fight personal battles. They convert the microphone and the podium to offensive assault weapons.

Aggressive humor is almost always offensive—in both meanings of the word. It antagonizes and it attacks.

I heard a business speaker once who was angry because he had gotten a citation while driving to the meetingplace. He wove his revenge into his presentation. He exhorted his listeners to set goals and establish priorities. "Don't be like the local police force. Don't be handing out traffic tickets while there are rapists and drug dealers roaming the streets."

He expected a laugh and a roar of "Hear, hear!" from the crowd. He got disapproval. It wasn't appropriate for him as a luncheon speaker to be fighting his private wars. Besides, how could this audience side with him when they didn't know any of the facts? If he was driving through their neighborhood at 80 miles an hour, he deserved the ticket. His sarcastic remarks aimed at their police were offensive.

It annoyed the audience because they realized they were being used to fight a personal battle—a battle that shouldn't involve them. They resented being forced to stand in the schoolyard while the speaker shouted names at his foe.

It may be all right to become offensive if you're the spokesman for your listeners in a common cause. In the preceding chapter we learned how a columnist attacked with humor and won a battle with the city leaders over potholes in the street. Everybody in the neighborhood wanted those holes fixed. This writer was verbalizing a common complaint. It was a community fight, not a personal vendetta.

As a speaker, you have an obligation to your listeners. They resent it when you use their time to attack windmills that only you see.

2. Humor that divides your audience: One of the sweetest sounds in the world (for humorists, anyway) is an explosion of laughter from an audience. The entire crowd laughs on cue. A humorist wants to entertain the entire audience; a speaker wants to enlighten the entire audience. So avoid anything that will divide your listeners.

Don't let your humor begin a mini-civil war, dividing brother against brother. Don't use anecdotes that set Democrats against Republicans, management against labor, men against women.

At a company retirement banquet I heard an upper management speaker praise the guest of honor for his loyalty during a recent strike. He said, "Not too long ago you could throw a rolled-up paper across the office and the only persons you would hit would be exempt employees and Good Old Charlie."

Awkward silence followed. The remark wasn't fair to either Good Old Charlie or the audience. It wasn't really meant to praise Charlie. There were better ways to do that. It was there to get a little dig in at the union. And it did.

It also resurrected all the animosity of the recent strike. It recalled the bitterness between the strikers and the executives. It even reminded everyone that Good Old Charlie was a "scab" in the minds of many of his fellow workers.

Divisive humor doesn't serve the speaker, either. It creates a tension that distracts an audience. You want people to pay attention to your remarks, hear them, and remember them. Separate your listeners into two or more factions and rather than accepting your words, their minds will be busy formulating their rebuttal.

Surely, you've relived an unpleasant encounter in your own mind. Someone annoyed you with an obnoxious remark, then you spent a good portion of your day fantasizing. "I should have said this or that." "Boy, if he had only done this, I would have done that." You're distracted. Your mind can't see the present for reconstructing the past. That's what happens to an audience when you divide. They don't listen to your words because they're too busy speaking their own inside their heads.

Divisive comedy also irritates a portion of your audience. They like you less than when you started. Rather than hearing your message and analyzing it, they begin looking for flaws in your argument. They search for reasons to disbelieve what you say. No speaker wants that.

But don't political humorists like Bob Hope and Johnny Carson divide the audience? When they do a joke about a Democratic president, don't they lose the Republicans? Not necessarily, because they're not really taking sides. They joke about authority, about the office of President. If a Republican gets elected, they'll kid him while he's in office. If a Democrat wins the election, he'll be kidded just the same.

That's a good example, though, of how humor and the attitude behind it can either be fun or divisive. Most of us forgive Hope and Carson for their comments about a liberal politician. But if a Bill Buckley made the same comment about a liberal, it would be offensive.

3. Humor that destroys your dignity: You've seen this shtick dozens of times: a comic takes a gulp of water, turns to speak to the audience, and the water dribbles out of his mouth, down his chin, and onto his shirt and tie. It gets a laugh.

The Three Stooges poked eyes, pulled hair, and pounded each other on top of the head.

Gallagher, a bright comedian, ends his act by smashing food with a sledge hammer. The big finale is a watermelon squashing. Fans bring clear plastic sheets so they can sit in the front rows without getting splashed.

Very few CEO's use these gimmicks.

Any humor you use in a business speech that lessens your dignity might be costly. The fun content of your presentation is supposed to help the audience receive it. If instead, they lose respect for the speaker, the message will be hurt. People won't trust or respect you and your credibility will be damaged.

Picture yourself in an emergency with a group of others. Who would you select as your leader? A person of quiet wit or the guy who tries to impress young ladies by removing his dentures and swallowing his nose with his lower lip?

Physical, slapstick comedy is not the only way you can diminish your dignity. Off-color jokes can do it; sick jokes can do it; almost anything in bad taste can do it. Say and do only those things that are consistent with your stature.

Not all physical comedy is undesirable for the business speaker. I once saw an awards presenter effectively use an ancient piece of comedy business. He presented a rose to a young woman. When she took the step to accept, the presenter kept the rose, and she held only the stem. It got a big laugh. He explained, "This is just like our travel expenses. The accounting department gives us most of it, but what they hold back is critical." He then presented the rose to the woman. It was physical humor, but pleasant and tasteful.

Tastefulness is the key. See and hear yourself doing your humor as a person in the audience might see and hear you. Then judge for yourself: when you watch and listen, are you proud of it? Do you maintain your dignity? If you don't, or you're not sure, don't do it.

People don't enjoy buffoonery, except when professional clowns and comics do it. It's demeaning. It insults their intelligence for a speaker to think they would enjoy this type of comedy.

The comment I heard most often about the Academy Awards telecast of 1988 focuses on this issue. Emcee Chevy Chase introduced Paul Newman as one of the presenters. When Newman reached the lectern, Chase chatted with him for a moment or two. They discussed the dignity of this affair and how prestigious an evening it was. When

Chevy Chase turned the lectern over to Paul Newman, he took about five steps and his pants fell down.

Paul Newman looked at him standing there in his shorts and said, "I suppose there's something to be said for comedy."

People I spoke to, remarked, "How could he do that to Paul Newman?" Newman added some class to the evening, and this shtick detracted from it.

When you step on the podium, you should add class to the proceedings. That's an important part of the image you need to convey to your listeners. That's prerequisite to their respecting you and listening to your remarks. Anything that detracts from your dignity lessens the impact of your speech.

4. Humor that embarrasses your audience (or any member of your audience): I once attended a convention where a featured speaker was an image coordinator. He taught business men and women how to dress properly and fashionably for the office, for travel, and so on. He was scheduled to speak at various times during the convention, and most people were planning to attend his sessions. Everyone wants to dress impressively and correctly.

I was there for his first speech, and it was quite crowded. He brought about a dozen men and women onstage and asked the audience to look at them for awhile and silently analyze how they were dressed. Were they dressed attractively? Did they inspire confidence? Would they make a good impression on clients?

After the audience evaluated them, he did. He took each person individually and critiqued his or her outfit.

He pointed out that one man was wearing a polyester sports jacket. He said, "The best thing about this jacket is that it will never burn. The worst thing about this jacket is that it will never burn." He advised that the jacket should be burned and then pointed out everything that was wrong with the jacket. It was cheap; it was outdated; it was tacky; it was unfashionable. He even added as a final insult, "A Nehru jacket might be preferable."

He wanted to be funny. Was he? Well, there were scattered laughs throughout the audience, nervous laughs. But he wasn't funny to the man in the polyester jacket. He wasn't funny to the friends of the man in the polyester jacket. He wasn't funny to most of the audience who sympathized with the man in the polyester jacket.

He embarrassed the volunteer onstage and a good percentage of the listeners. It got worse.

He told one woman her dress was fashionable and perfect for travel, "if you're accompanying your husband across the plains in a covered wagon."

The next time he spoke, few people were in the audience. Curiosity prompted most of those who did attend. They wanted to see if this man was as horrendous as everyone said he was.

He frightened listeners away for two reasons: they were afraid of being singled out for ridicule, and they didn't want to see others embarrassed.

This man's message was good. He offered invaluable tips about fashion, colors, materials, how to shop for clothing, prices to pay, and plenty of other useful information. After that first session, however, no one wanted to hear it. Wait, let me change that: They still wanted to hear it; but they didn't want to hear it from him.

Those who did hear it, rejected it. The man quickly became so unlikable onstage that no one would listen to what he had to say. Even though he was right, they refused to accept it.

We could come to his defense. We could say that those who stepped onstage, volunteering for a critique, were inviting negative comments. Of course, they were. They probably expected errors in their ensemble and wanted him to point this out. There is a way to offer constructive criticism, though, without embarrassing and alienating your audience. It can be done safely with humor.

I have seen another speaker, a very successful business lecturer, who invites members of her audience onstage to become contestants in a male beauty pageant. She is a former Miss America contestant, and she wants the men in her audience to feel what that is like.

Her purpose is not to embarrass these men, but to have fun with them. She teases them, tricks them into making dumb mistakes, asks them foolish questions, and then points out the foolishness of their answers. The men enjoy themselves and so does the audience.

What's the difference? First, she checks with her potential "beauty contestants." She warns them about the gimmick. She doesn't rehearse them or tell them specifically what she will say or do—the whole thing is spontaneous—but she does tell them that she will tease and kid them. She seeks outgoing men. Those who would rather not participate can just say so.

Second, her kidding is harmless. Some of it is insulting, but as we saw in an earlier chapter, you can insult without offending.

Third, her humor is generalized, not specific. The person in her presentation is not singled out for a vicious attack. He's the representative of the audience. The audience senses that whatever she is saying to him, she could just as well be saying to them. Whatever she tricks him into, she could have tricked the audience into, also. When they laugh at him, they laugh at themselves. "There but for the grace of God, go I," they might say.

Fourth, her attitude is important. The show is fun. It has a message, but the humor content is fun. Her attitude says to her volunteers, "We're going to have a good time up here. I like you, and when we're done, I'm sure you'll like me." The audience senses that and none of her joking embarrasses anyone.

Unlike our earlier example, this speaker attracts more and bigger audiences. When people hear how much fun her show is, they want to attend and participate.

Beware of embarrassing your audience. It's not only onstage participation that can do it. Stories, anecdotes, and comments can humiliate, too. If you ridicule a person at the head table without good cause, you can lose your audience. Blue material can embarrass an audience. They may laugh the nervous laugh, but many of them won't want to see you again.

5. Humor that hurts: We've already discussed insult humor and how to use it without offending. However, there are other ways of hurting people with comedy and not all of them are foreseeable. For instance, I once did a show with a comic who liked to use aggressive humor. When he went into the audience for some questions-and-answers, he said to a young man in a striped tee shirt, "Oh, look, here's a kid who's dressed like a pirate."

The "pirate" was a guest of one of our writers, who told us later that the young man was very upset by the remark. He didn't understand why this comedian was calling him a pirate.

How do you protect against that? Well, sometimes you don't—you can't. All you can do is review the humor content of your speech and be aware of your audience. If you know something will hurt, take it out. If you are not sure, replace it anyway.

CHAPTER TWELVE

Humor in the Workplace

A writing friend of mine had a unique criteria for accepting or rejecting freelance assignments. He'd caution himself, "If it ain't fun, don't do it." It was an effective, if ungrammatical, philosophy for him, but for most of us it's hardly practical.

In the 40-hour-a-week/50-week-a-year world, we don't have that kind of control over which assignments we land, or what sort of headaches come with each assignment. However, we can amend that writer's advice: "If it ain't fun, make it fun."

We spend about a third of our lives in the workplace. With a little effort, we can make it as pleasant as the other two-thirds of our life. We can use our humor and our sense of humor just as effectively to benefit ourselves as we can in our communications to benefit our audience.

Can humor change the facts? Can it transform a negative to a positive? No. But nothing is totally negative or totally positive. And, as the song says, it helps to "accentuate the positive and eliminate the negative."

How can we use humor every day in the workplace?

First, we can be aware of its power. Humor is an attitude, an outlook; a thinking process. We can control our thinking. But we have to remember to do it, and often we have to make a conscious effort to do it.

Most success philosophies stress that our thoughts control our behavior. *Think and Grow Rich* was Napoleon Hill's best-selling title. *The Magic of Believing* was Claude Bristol's. Norman Vincent Peale wrote *The Power of Positive Thinking*. They all say we are what we think. Think happy and we become happier.

Bob Hope told me a story that illustrates this. He was travelling with his radio troupe during World War II. They were broadcasting from various battle zones, entertaining the troops. While they were flying from one base to another on a military plane, officers advised them to put on their life jackets.

The plane was in trouble and the crew thought they might have to make a forced landing on water. Hope said that there was fear and anxiety on everyone's face—except for Jerry Colonna's. When Hope looked at him, Colonna just shrugged his shoulders and made a face that said, "I might as well put the jacket on. There's not much else I can do about it."

Hope told me that Colonna's reaction was so unexpected, and the face he made so hilarious that, despite the crisis, everyone laughed. The rubber-faced comedian wanted to lighten the situation and he did.

"It just snapped us all out of it," Hope said. The emergency still existed, but the morale improved because of Colonna's attitude.

The aircraft landed safely, but this incident must have made a deep impression on Hope. He told me the story over 40 years after it happened.

That story points out another benefit of a sense of humor—it's catching. Colonna's attitude affected the others.

It's the opposite of a vicious circle. Humor creates a pleasant atmosphere, which makes everyone else more pleasant, which makes it easier for us to be pleasant.

Second, we can keep focused on the present. Most worry goes on when we fictionalize or fantasize about imaginary problems, or magnify real problems. In stress most of us aggravate the trouble by projecting the worst possible scenario. We create or manufacture difficulties in our minds.

In the example above, there was a threat of a crash landing, but there wasn't a crash.

Humor is truth—it's reality. It enables us to see and react to what is happening, not what might happen or what could happen.

Life is much easier if we deal with the challenge that's confronting us, not with the one we create.

When I was scheduled for heart surgery a few years ago, I was frightened. The doctor told me that I was an excellent candidate for the surgery and that he expected no problems. But I expected problems. I worried about every unpleasant contingency, regardless of how unlikely.

Phyllis Diller called to cheer me up. I was determined to be uncheerable. She told me of many friends who had the same surgery and were revitalized. She told me that I'd be up and around in no time at all and feeling better than ever.

I said, "Phyllis, I know what you're saying, but I'm still scared." Phyllis, who kids herself about her many cosmetic surgeries, said, "Gene, just look on it as a chest lift."

I like the story of the cowboy in the old west who knew how to view things with a sense of reality and a sense of humor.

He was enjoying some drinks and a few hands of poker with some friends in the town saloon when a fierce desperado barged in. The villain drew his guns and shouted, "I want every yellow-bellied, snake-livered, slime-crawling, chicken-hearted, son of a sidewinder to clear out of here, or I'm gonna start shooting."

Chairs scraped on the floor, tables overturned, and patrons scrambled for the exits. The only one who remained was our hero.

The outlaw walked over to him, shoved his gun under his nose and repeated, "I said I wanted every yellow-bellied, snake-livered, slime-crawling, chicken-hearted, son of a sidewinder to clear out of here."

The cowboy said, "I heard you. There sure were a lot of them, weren't there?"

PART III

The Humor of Business

*"There is no good reason why a joke should
not be appreciated more than once.
Imagine how little good music there
would be if, for example, a conductor
refused to play Beethoven's Fifth Symphony
on the ground that his audience might have
heard it before."*

A. P. Herbert

ABSENTEEISM

We have a lot of absenteeism in our office. Well, I guess it's more correct to say we have a lot of absenteeism *not* in our office.

We have a fellow in our office who accumulates a lot of absenteeism. I said to the boss one day, "Why don't you fire him?" He said, "Fire him? I don't even know what he looks like."

If he had been a cartoon character, the movie would have been called *Snow White and the Six Dwarfs*.

I'll give you an idea how often he shows up at work. His nickname around the office is "Halley's Comet."

He's so undependable. He's never there when you need him. In fact, he's never there when you don't need him, either.

He shows up at the office maybe once a week . . . just to pull the weeds from his parking space.

He takes a sick day any time he feels like it. We don't send him a get-well card; we send him a get-real card.

I'll tell you, if they gave out awards for absenteeism, this guy would not be there to receive his.

This gentleman finally retired. He can stay at home now on his own time.

He had a very big turnout at his retirement party. So many of his coworkers were anxious to meet him.

This guy was absent so much we held his retirement party at his house.

When he finally retired, the boss said, "I don't know what we'll ever do without you . . . although we've had years and years of practice."

He gave a nice speech at his retirement ceremony. He said, "I'm going to miss my coworkers . . . whoever you are."

AIR-CONDITIONING WARS

In our office there's a constant feud between those who want the office warmer and those who want it colder. We call it the war between the Sweat-Hogs and the Blue Lippers.

They're constantly raising and lowering the temperature. We have the only thermostat in the building that goes up and down more often than the lobby elevator.

The "coldies" hate the "hotties." They call them the Underarm Stainers.

The "hotties" hate the "coldies." They call them the Icicle Nosers.

One guy in our office always wants the air-conditioner turned up higher. He was trying to adjust the thermostat the other day, and a fellow worker hit him with a snowball.

Some people want the workplace too cold. Last year our office had 21 sick days due to frostbite.

You know it's too cold in there when the office watercooler turns into an ice-maker.

They keep it so cold in our office we had to call the exterminator. We had a penguin problem.

It's always cold in our office. The boss likes the thermostat set to the same temperature as his heart.

You know it's cold in our office when we have a vending machine that serves coffee, tea, and hot whale blubber.

Some people want the office warmer and warmer. They literally want to earn their salary by the sweat of their brow.

One guy keeps the office hot because he can never get warm enough. The other day he put on a second sweater. His first one melted.

AMBITION

Ambition is the desire to get what you deserve. Reckless ambition is the desire to get what you deserve whether you deserve it or not.

We have a guy in our office who wants to be a prince so badly he's spent his whole life kissing frogs and a few other things.

In our office he was known as The Man Who Wanted to Be King. And everybody wanted to crown him.

This guy's problem was that he was so full of ambition there wasn't any room left for competence.

This guy said, "I want to get ahead." I said, "Good. That's better than what you have sitting on top of your neck now."

Talk about ruthless ambition. This guy would scratch, claw, and step all over his friends for a lateral move.

This gentleman always wanted to move ahead. When he was a child he wanted to be his own parent.

He's very arrogant. He considers his peers beneath him.

This guy was ruthless. He has very few friends, but a vast array of former friends.

He wanted power to impress his friends. When he finally got the power, he had no one left to impress.

He wanted the world on a string. All of his coworkers wanted him on a stick.

It was always safer to turn your back on this guy. That way you wouldn't get a foot in your face as he stepped over you.

BEEPERS

My boss tried to talk me into wearing a beeper. He said, "Do you realize if you have a beeper I can reach you anytime I want to?" I said, "Is that your question or my answer?"

I dislike beepers because they always go off when I don't want them to . . . like in this lifetime.

I told the boss I didn't like beepers because they interfered with my life. The boss said, "Don't kid me. With the salary I pay, you can't afford a life."

The boss wanted me to wear a beeper. He said, "What should I do if I want to talk to you on the weekend?" I said, "Be my caddy."

The boss said, "Beepers are very simple to wear. You just put them on your belt." I said, "No thanks. My belt has enough to hold up already."

Beepers are unfair. You can be reached 24 hours a day for 8 hours' pay.

The boss said, "Beepers are no problem. Just slip it into your pocket." He knows with the money he pays, I sure have empty pockets available.

I don't like wearing a beeper. It's like the company putting you under house arrest.

The boss said, "You should be proud to wear a beeper. It shows you're an important member of the team." Remember the good old days when commensurate salary used to accomplish that?

The boss said, "When I need you, I'll beep you and then you call me." I said, "Why don't we cut out the middleman? I'll just call you anytime I have a need to be needed."

The boss said, "With a beeper I can reach you on the weekends." I said, "Why don't you just drive over to the house?" He said, "Suppose you're not home?" I said, "It doesn't matter. My beeper will be."

I told the boss I wouldn't wear a beeper. He said, "How else can I get you to come when I call you?" I said, "Send me to obedience school."

The thing I hate most about Monday is that it's followed by Tuesday, Wednesday, Thursday, and Friday.

BLUE MONDAY & T.G.I.F.

I don't know why they call it "Blue Monday." Generally on that morning, my eyes are a bright shade of pink.

Whoever invented Mondays made a big mistake . . . and they had the whole weekend to think about it.

Mondays are tough for me. I enjoy my weekends so much it's hard for me to give them up cold turkey.

Someday I'm going to buy myself an alarm clock that doesn't have a Monday on it.

There's a lot to be said for Monday morning—most of it unprintable.

I don't know who invented Fridays, but whoever it is should take the rest of the week off.

If there had been no such day as Friday, I would have had to invent it to keep my sanity.

Friday is nature's way of saying, "Eat, drink, and be merry because Monday you climb back into the harness again."

Friday is a beautiful day. I not only get a paycheck, but two whole days to spend it.

The worst thing about Friday is that even people who didn't do anything all week still get to enjoy it.

I generally fall down on my knees by my desk and say, "Thank God it's Friday." Unfortunately, I start doing that around Wednesday.

BUDGETS

My budget has more slashes in it than a sword fighter with a losing record.

Most of the time the boss won't give me the time of day. Around budget time, that's all he'll give me.

I asked the boss, "Have you reviewed my proposed budget?" He said, "Yeah. I like half of it."

At the budget meeting I said, "I'd like to put in my 2 cents' worth." The boss said, "You can't afford it."

A budget is like a waistline. You can cut it down, but you're not going to enjoy it.

It's difficult sometimes to tell fact from fiction . . . especially around budget time.

You can tell when it's budget time around the office. That's when your boss comes to work in the shape of the word "No."

You know your budget is in trouble when your boss says to his secretary on the intercom, "Send the next person in along with another dozen red pencils."

Budget meetings are tough. That's when the boss cuts both you and your budget down to size.

I told my boss, "You can't get blood from a rock." The boss said, "Don't worry about it. We're cutting your rock down to a pebble."

I told the boss, "Here's my list of reasons why I can't run my department on this budget." The boss said, "Well, here's my list of people who can."

Everybody has budget problems. I told the boss, "I need a bigger budget or I'm outta here." The boss said, "If I give you a bigger budget, *I'm* outta here."

Budget time—that's when your boss goes around the office all day singing, "Anything I can do, you can do cheaper."

Budget time is when you take "what you want" and reduce it to "what you need" so your boss can cut it all the way down to "what you're gonna get."

Submitting a budget is like singing "Row, Row, Row Your Boat"—no matter how many times you sing it, you always wind up back at the beginning again.

BUSINESS CARDS

I always give my business card to everyone I meet. I find people appreciate them, except for those people who were expecting a tip.

I just came back from a business convention. I came back with some good information, a few prospects, and 5,427 new business cards.

A good business card should have printed on it who you are, what you do, and a notice that reads, "If you throw this in any wastebasket you'll have 18 years of bad luck."

After most business conventions I always call up all the people that I received business cards from. I say to them, "Excuse me for bothering you, but did I leave my shoes in your room?"

I always carry several hundred business cards with me. It helps people remember me. They say, "Oh yeah, he's the guy with the bulging pockets."

Give a business card to every business associate you meet. It helps people remember you, helps them locate you, and it's the only way to get rid of the doggone things.

Salespeople collect business cards as potential customers. Anything else that multiplies that fast is considered either a nuisance or an epidemic.

"I'll give you my business card and you give me yours. That way we'll both have something to throw away once we get back to our rooms."

I always carry business cards to conventions. Sometimes, after visiting the hospitality suite it's the only way I can remember who I am and who I work for.

Sometimes I feel business cards do absolutely no good, yet everybody uses them. They're like paper umbrellas in a $4 drink.

Nowadays you have to list your name, business association, address, phone number, fax number, E-mail number. We're either going to have to make business cards larger or eyesight better.

In order to drum up business, my optometrist has all his business cards printed blurry.

BUSINESS DRESS

Men have it easier dressing for success. Do you know how hard it is to climb the corporate ladder in pantyhose and heels?

I told my boss if he wanted me to abide by the dress code, he was going to have to update it a bit. I don't mind having to wear a dress and respectable shoes, but I refuse to wear a bustle.

People tell us we should dress for success. I don't know about you, but my idea of being successful also involves being comfortable.

My boss wants us to dress for success, but he only pays for mediocrity.

I tried dressing for success once. It clashed with the rest of my life.

My boss said he wanted us to dress the way the company was run. I had to run out and buy a whole new wardrobe. I didn't have one cheap thing in my closet.

BUSINESS TRAVEL

I travel a lot in my work. I'll never forget what my boss said to me when he presented me with my 25-year pin. He said, "It's nice to meet you."

I'm always flying somewhere on my job. I think the only reason they hired me is because in an emergency my seat cushion could be used as a flotation device.

When I die I know I'm going to heaven. I certainly have enough frequent-flier miles to cover the trip.

I think I'm traveling too much for the company. I get better treatment at the airport than I do at the office.

I spend more time in the air than a buzzard with bunions.

My right arm is now 4 inches longer than my left from lugging my suitcase through airports.

I'm one step above a frequent flier. I'm listed as an incessant flier.

I think I travel too much for the company. My wife gave the children explicit instructions: "Don't ever talk to strangers . . . unless he happens to be your father."

You've heard the expression "A man's home is his castle"? For me, it's just a laundry drop.

We're not sure which it is. Either the company sends me to all the trouble spots, or anywhere the company sends me becomes a trouble spot.

I spend so much time on the road I have to file an absentee ballot all the time. Not to vote—to make family decisions.

I did manage to watch my daughter perform in a school play. But my wife had to point out which one she was.

CHEAP BOSS

I have the cheapest boss in the world. He goes over expense accounts with a fine-tooth comb and then charges you for the comb.

Expense to him is a four-letter word.

Every November he becomes an atheist so he won't have to send out Christmas cards.

He insists that we all travel as cheaply as possible. If he ran an airline, he'd make the pilot fly coach.

When we travel he not only wants us to give the company our frequent-flier bonuses, but also the mint that the hotel leaves on our pillow.

He said to me once, "Why do you want to leave the company?" I said, "I don't want to leave; I just asked for a raise." He said, "Same thing."

I've known people who are so cheap they write on both sides of a sheet of paper. He tries to write on both sides of the computer screen.

He even hates to waste paper. Our planning department does their preliminary drawings on an Etch-a-Sketch.

Once I was a half hour late and he docked me a full hour's pay. He said it was one half hour of *my* time and a half hour of *his* time because he couldn't work, worrying about how late I would be.

Every time he watches "A Christmas Carol," he considers Ebenezer Scrooge a turncoat.

At 25-year parties, he gives the guests of honor a price list . . . in case they want to buy themselves a 25-year pin.

At business lunches, when the check arrives, he's always the first to put his hand into his pocket . . . then leave it there.

When he hands out his business card, he always asks people to return it when they're done with it.
. . . if they don't, he bills them.

My boss can squeeze a nickel so hard that the buffalo on it speaks with a high-pitched voice.

My boss took me out for coffee and doughnuts the other day. It was a unique experience. It's the first time I've ever given blood.

CHEAP HOTELS

Our company sends us to some pretty cheap hotels. You've heard of four-star hotels? These are forewarned.

Our company sends us to cheap hotels. Usually, the honeymoon suite is the room with a door on it.

Our company patronizes very low-class, inexpensive hotels. You can pay for your room with cash, credit card, or "Don't tell the police about us."

I was lucky, I got a room with a shower. Well, it's not really a shower. The roof leaked every time the guy upstairs took a bath.

Normally, you get your choice of a king- or queen-size bed. This hotel only had one size—peasant.

I called the front desk and said, "I just checked in and there's no closet in Room 316." They told me why. Room 316 used to be a closet.

They had smoking and nonsmoking rooms, which meant that they hadn't quite put the fire out yet.

After I checked in I called the desk and said, "Excuse me, but my bed only has one pillow on it." And they said, "Oh, so you're the one who has it!"

They made my bed every morning. That's because every night I slept in it, it broke.

When I checked in I asked, "Do you have a nice restaurant in this hotel?" The clerk said, "We think we do, but the Board of Health has yet to go along with us."

They advertise a maid service that's "Just like your own home." The maid comes in and nags you until you clean up your own room.

You're guaranteed fresh towels every day. That's because none of the facilities—not the sink, the tub, or the shower—is in working order.

I requested a room with a view, so they put me on the fourth floor. It's a three-story hotel.

The rooms are very small. I asked if someone could help me with my luggage. They said, "If you bring your luggage up to the room, there won't be room for you."

The bellhop was also the guy who delivers room service. So he won't bring your luggage up until it's ice cold.

COWORKERS

One guy in our office is a lazy worker and proud of it. He knows he does nothing, but he does it so well.

He's the only guy I know who can put his shoulder to the wheel and his nose to the grindstone and take a nap in that position.

He tries to get out of as much work as he can. The boss told us once we all had to pull our own weight, so he went on a diet.

This guy does nothing at work. He could just as easily stay home all day except he hates to give up his coffee breaks.

He insists there are only *six* deadly sins. He considers sloth a virtue.
. . . he also considers it his job description.

He does absolutely nothing all day long. Some days he does less than nothing. He says it gives him a leg up on the next day.

Another coworker is very slow. When you ask him if he's got a minute, it takes him a minute and a half to decide.

I've been on business trips with him and noticed that he even sits on an airplane slow.

One worker in our office is very meticulous. He does crossword puzzles in the typewriter.

This guy is careful about everything. He dots all his "i's" and crosses all his "t's" . . . even when there are not "i's" or "t's" in the word.

The man is compulsive about organization. He eats alphabet soup in alphabetical order.

COMMITTEES

Committees are when one person who doesn't know the answer appoints ten or twelve other people who don't know the answer to come up with the answer.

Committees are when a group of people say, "Let's meet once a month and convince ourselves that we still haven't found a solution."

They say that two heads are better than one, but no heads are better than a committee.

Some committees not only never find a solution, they never really define the problem.

If at first you don't succeed, appoint a committee to take the pressure off yourself.

I was on one committee that met every Tuesday for 6 weeks in a row trying to decide if it wasn't better to hold the meetings on Thursdays.

Committees should always have one strong executive in charge for the same reason that a bus only has one steering wheel.

An executive who always says, "I'll appoint a committee to study the situation" is like a father who always says, "Go ask your mother."

You show me a committee that can't come up with the solution to a problem, and I'll form a committee to find out why.

I like the honesty of one committee report. They said, "We have met the problem head-on and discovered that we're it."

Our Committee on Quality Control finally issued their report, but all the pages came out blurry.

COMMUTING

Traffic was really bad today. There was one stretch of about a half hour where I traveled at only five miles an hour. The car traveled at three.

The worst thing about a tough commute to work is that when you finally get it over with, you're at work.

The commute was horrible today. I made the entire trip from home to work without once leaving the scene of the accident.

Cars were packed tightly on the roads today. The couple ahead of me were necking the whole way. She was in a Buick; he was in a Toyota.

Traffic was jammed together today. I ran out of gas and didn't notice it until the car behind me pulled off the freeway.

I never saw cars packed that close. I signaled for a left-hand turn and the guy in the car next to me bit my finger.

"The freeway was so packed today I got off at the McCormick off-ramp."
"Wait a minute. There is no McCormick off-ramp."
"There is now."

Cars were packed together on the road today. The guy in the car ahead of me kept shaking his head no. Then I figured out it was because his hair was caught in my windshield wipers.

This morning's commute was stop-and-go the entire way. Which was good. Normally it's just "stop."

I enjoyed a pleasant commute to work this morning. Pleasant commute—that means I finished with the same car I started in.

Traffic's always jammed on the route I take to and from work. I replace bumpers on my car more often than I do tires.

My commute this morning was relatively traffic free . . . then I pulled out of my driveway.

COMPANY PICNIC

It's easy to spot the boss at the company picnic. He's the one wearing Bermuda shorts and a tie.

We have our company picnic on Sunday, which cuts down on the attendance. Even the ants won't come unless they get time and a half.

I knew I was in trouble at the company picnic. My tuna-fish sandwich was wrapped in a pink slip.

I was so excited that everyone wanted me on their team for the tug-of-war. My boss said, "Of course, it's the only time so much dead weight comes in handy."

They had pony rides at our annual company picnic, which was fitting. You spend hours going round and round and never really get anywhere.
. . . and you always have to be careful where you step.

COMPUTERS

The big difference between computers and humans is that computers can't think, . . . but they know it.

Computers are smart. You give them bad instructions, they print out an error message. You give most workers bad instructions, they do it anyway.

We used to look for a worker with a good head on his shoulders. Now we settle for a worker with a good computer on his desk.

They're predicting that someday computers will think for themselves. They used to say that about executives, too.

My computer crashed the other day. That's because I got so frustrated by it I pushed it out a window.

Computers are very fast. That means I can now make 200 times the mistakes I used to make doing it by hand.

It's not the computer that makes a difference. It's how you use it. That's pretty much the way it used to be with your head.

The business world is getting used to the speed at which computers work. At our company we now get 38 seconds for lunch.

I don't know how my computer works, I just know it does. The boss says the same thing about me.

I dislike computers. I hate having something sitting on my desk that's more efficient and more productive than I am.
. . . and is better cared for, too.

The motto of our Computer Department is "Garbage in; garbage out." Times change. That used to be the motto of our Personnel Department.

CONVENTIONS

The motto at most conventions: "Eat, drink, and be merry because the next vacation you take may not be paid for by the company."

Conventions are a hospitality suite surrounded by some sort of meetings.

The boss asked me, "What did you come home from the convention with?" I answered, "A hangover and someone else's trousers."

There is a lot of work done at most business conventions—by the people who clean up the hospitality suites.

I endorse name tags at all conventions. I've been to some where I couldn't remember who the hell I was.

I was at one company convention where everyone attended a rodeo. It was educational. Many of the people in the company had never seen a complete horse.

I attended a convention for a company that was doing so badly that instead of reading the annual financial report, they had a moment of silence.

I carry two suitcases to all conventions. One for my clothing and one to carry my business cards.

At one convention a motivational speaker told his audience, "You people can do anything you want." So, they all got up and left.

A convention is a golf tournament surrounded by cocktail parties with a meeting or two thrown in for the obsessively conscientious.

The boss said, "I'm sending you to the convention in Hawaii, but I want you to learn something." I learned that four mai-tais before dinner is my limit.
. . . I also learned how to say "I'm entitled to one phone call" in Hawaiian.

CUSTOMERS

My customers forced me out of my last business venture. I didn't have any.

You show me a business person who has nothing but happy customers, and I'll show you a business person who isn't charging enough.

If the customer is always right, why don't we hire them instead of employees?

I'll never forget the pep talk we all got from one of our managers. He said, "Forget customers. Just go out and get more business."

Customers would be the scourge of the business world except for one thing: They're the ones with the money.

Let's face it: We're all in business to make money. Both the product and the customer are just necessary evils.

That saying, "The customer is always right," is always annoying.

The customer is always right . . . until the check clears and the warranty runs out.

I knew one business person who had the right idea. He always spelled the word *customer* with a dollar sign in front of it.

I had trouble with one client. He said, "I thought the customer was always right." I said, "The customer *was* always right until you came along."
. . . "You've loused up a perfect record."

DECISION-MAKING

Am I a good decision-maker? The answer to that is yes . . . maybe.

Some people don't understand how tough decision-making can be. Sometimes it's the difference between yes and no, or between employed and unemployed.

Making decisions at the office is much more difficult than making them at home. At the office I have to weigh the pros and cons, discover the effects on productivity, and take into account office morale. At home I just have to agree with my spouse.

When I was promoted to manager I made a very big decision.
. . . I was going to hire someone else to make all the decisions.

When making a decision, you want to surround yourself with information, facts, and someone else to blame.

DULL COWORKER

One guy who works in our office is so dull that when I call him, I actually prefer talking to the answering machine.

This guy is very dull. He likes to ride elevators because the music turns him on.

It's more exciting to watch snail races than to spend time in his company.

He's been registered with the bureau of missing personalities for years.

The first thing people say when they're introduced to him is, "I'm sorry I didn't catch your name. I dozed off."

He has the charm and charisma of a dinner roll.

He has all the warmth and vivacity of a "Thank You for Not Smoking" sign.

What's he like at a party? Nobody knows. Wherever he is, there's no party.

He had the 24-hour virus once for 48 hours. It stayed an extra day because they had so much in common.

He's a terrible conversationalist. Even when he has nothing to say, he has trouble finding the words.

His idea of a good time is to go out with some friends and paint the town beige.

When he was born, the doctor slapped his bottom, and it's the most excitement he's had so far.

I'll give you an idea how dull this guy is. His favorite color is khaki.

He came to me one day and asked, "Can I talk to you?" I said, "Sure. I need the sleep."

DUMB BOSS

I work for the dumbest boss in the world. When the good Lord was giving out brains, he thought they said "grains" and said, "Make mine oatmeal."

Actually, he has a good brain. Well, he should. It has hardly ever been used.

Every time my boss goes to the gas station, he fills the car, checks the oil, cleans the windshield, and gets a little extra air for his head.

It's trouble working for a boss who's this dumb. Do you realize how hard it is to cash a paycheck written in crayon?

He has a Ph.D., which we think stands for "Philled with Dumbness."

You can always tell when my boss is thinking. His toes curl up.

He once boasted to us about his office chair: "I want to have the softest seat in the whole company because that's where I do all my thinking."

He has the mentality of about a nine-year-old. He begins every staff meeting with a game of Pin the Tail on the Donkey.

He has a whole series of management books written by Dr. Seuss.

He once gave us a peptalk on punctuality and finished with: "Even if you're taking the day off, I want you to be absent on time."

If he had been a dodo bird, they would have become extinct years and years earlier.

He thinks he's bilingual because he only speaks English, but thinking is foreign to him.

I said to him one day, "Why did God make dumb bosses like you?" He answered, "So there'd be someone to hire people like you."

The only way he can remember his shoe size is that it's the same as his I.Q.

When they were giving out brains, he thought they said "drains" and said, "Give me one that's not clogged with anything."

EXPENSE ACCOUNTS

Even though it clearly states "Travel Expenses" at the top of the form, many of us fill it out as if it reads "Unofficial Christmas Bonus."

The boss said, "I got your expense account. It has more padding than the Green Bay Packers."

The boss said, "We're going to give you a generous expense account because we don't want *you* to pay for anything unnecessarily. But just remember, neither do *we*."

I submit an expense account as if my company were Santa Claus.
. . . unfortunately, I didn't remember that they make a list, and they check it twice.
. . . they sure found out who was naughty and nice.
. . . which means I'm getting a lump of coal instead of a reimbursement this month.

I'm very ethical about my expense accounts. Whenever I overcharge the company, I give 10 percent of it to charity.

My mother used to tell me that in some parts of the world people have to go to bed each night without a padded expense account.

I complained to the boss that I didn't get a bonus this year. He said, "Yes, you did. Reread some of the expense accounts you submitted."

I pad my expense account so much that it look like the bra of the girl I took to the senior prom.
. . . which was the last time I paid for everything out of my own pocket.

The boss called me into a meeting and said, "Would you get your expense-account folder, please? It's in the filing cabinet under *F* for 'fiction.'"

The boss summoned me into his office and said, "I've got good news for you. The Accounting Department called; your expense accounts won this year's award for Mystery Writing."

FILING

We have a Lost-and-Found Department in our office. Unfortunately, it's our filing system.

Filing is a way of finding something when you need it. At our office we use "reverse filing." If you should happen to find something, search for a reason to need it.

I fired one assistant because he was incompetent at filing. He claimed his contract forbade termination, but none of us could find it.

We have a series of filing drawers labeled from "A" to "Z" and then one other drawer labeled "IHS." That stands for "In Here Somewhere."

My mother always said, "If you put things away when you're done with them, you'll always be able to find them again." My mother had a different secretary than I have.

My secretary took his filing system and put it into the computer. Now we can't find the computer.

My assistant devised a very complicated filing system. He said, "I can find anything you want. Just give me 3 days' notice." So I gave him 3 days to find a new job.

I'm worried about my new assistant's filing ability. The two drawers in his filing cabinet are labeled "A to 20" and "21 to Z."

My new assistant said his mother told him, "You always find things in the last place you'd look." So that's where he files them.

My new assistant couldn't find the "Aardvark" file. I said, "Look under 'extinct animals.'" He said, "The aardvark's not extinct." I said, "It will be by the time you find the file."

A good filing system finds what you're looking for exactly where you're looking for it. A bad filing system finds what you're not looking for exactly where what you're looking for should be.

My assistant has such a convoluted filing system that no one else can find anything. He said, "I'm the only one who can put my finger on anything in this office." I said, "Here. Put it on this hot plate."

GETTING FIRED

I was an editor for a company that published a thesaurus. When I was fired, they gave me a choice of 48 different words that I could call it.

Once the boss called me in and said, "All good things must come to an end, and today, you're one of them."

I worked for a man once who was too gentle to fire anyone. What he would do was give them a day off and then move the company to a new location.

My manager called me in one day and told me to clean out my desk. I said, "If you're going to give me that much work to do, why don't you just fire me?"

I worked in Quality Control once and I got a pink slip in my envelope that said, "You're being terminated."

The boss handed me my severance pay and said, "This is the first check you've really earned since you've been here."

The boss said, "Today I'm giving you 2 weeks' notice." I asked, "I'm being fired? Tell me why." He said, "I can't. That would take 3 weeks."

The boss sat me down and said, "I've never enjoyed firing anyone . . . until today."

I asked the boss, "Will you give me a letter of recommendation?" He said, "Gladly. I want you to work for our competitors."

I asked, "Why are you firing me? I didn't do anything." He said, "Why do you ask the question if you're going to answer it too?"

I asked, "You're firing me after all I've done for this company?" The boss said, "No, I'm firing you after all you've done *to* this company."

The boss said, "You're fired." I said, "You mean, I don't work here anymore?" He said, "You never worked here. That's why I mean you're fired."

GOLF

Golf is nothing but humility spread out over 18 holes.

I played with one business associate who said at the first tee, "I'm not a very good golfer." It's the only truthful thing he said through the next 18 holes.

I played golf with one customer. I said, "What's your handicap?" He said, "The rules of the game."

I played with one guy who cheated like crazy. After 9 holes he said, "I may break par today." I said, "Why not? You've broken every other rule connected with this game."

I've met a lot of interesting people playing golf. They were folks I met while asking for directions back to the golf course.

My boss plays a wild game of golf. He's the only player at his club who has to use a golf cart with four-wheel drive.

I went to my golf pro for some lessons. He looked at my swing and said, "I think the first thing we should teach you is how to survive in the woods for 3 days or more."

I asked my golf pro, "What do you think about my swing?" He said, "Whenever I see a swing like that, I try not to think about it."

I increased my chances of getting a promotion while playing golf. I sent three of the guys ahead of me on the organizational chart to the hospital.

It was on the golf course that my boss told me I was a "sycophantic, mealy-mouthed yes-man." I said, "If that's what you really think, then get someone else to be your caddy."

I played golf with a customer the other day and got his business. He said, "If you send out invoices like you keep score I'll expect a ten-percent discount on every shipment."

I played with a very wild golfer the other day. He didn't have to rent a golf cart. Where he hit the ball he could use public transportation.

HI-TECH

Remember: In the good old days when you made a phone call, a live person actually answered the phone.

Nowadays you get a cold, heartless, unthinking machine. I much prefer getting a cold, heartless, unthinking receptionist.

I made a phone call the other day and a real person did answer the phone. I hung up because I didn't know what buttons to push.

It's all answering machines or voice mail. In the course of my business communications I've probably made more recordings than Elvis Presley.

People are so used to voice mail. When I get sales calls on the phone, I say, "If you want information, press 1. If you want to purchase something, press 2. If you want to sell me something, press the button on the top of your phone." They do and hang themselves up.

We have a copier in our office that is so complicated anyone who can operate it is overqualified to work for us.

The boss asked me to copy a document, and I must have pushed the wrong button and got 320 copies. The boss asked, "Why did you make 320 copies?" I said, "I figured that way we'd have 160 copies each."

It's the only copy machine I've ever seen that you can't operate without a copilot.

It prints in four colors—all red.

When I want to make copies, I have to call someone for help. Which is difficult because I don't know how to operate the phones, either.

In fact, the only office accessory I feel qualified to operate is the watercooler.

Everything in our office beeps. Our office sounds like mating season for the Roadrunner.

JOB EVALUATION

I got my job evaluation today. It was stapled to a page of help-wanted ads.

Job evaluation—that's when the boss calls you into his office, sits you down, and puts you down.

I had a very simple job evaluation. The boss took me aside and left me there.

The boss asked if I had ever heard the expression "One rotten apple can spoil the barrel." I said, "Yes." He said, "Then stay away from the rest of my apples."

The boss said, "I'm unhappy with your work in this office." I said, "Small world, isn't it?"

I asked the boss at my job review, "Am I pulling my weight?" He said, "No, it's more like you're pushing your luck."

I got such a terrible job review that I said to the boss, "Why do you keep me?" He said, "It's a form of job security. You're doing so bad that it makes the rest of my workers look good."

I didn't mind the boss giving me a bad job review. What really ticked me off was when he proved it.

The boss said, "You're working at about 50 percent of your potential. Why?" I said, "Because that's what you're paying me."

The boss opened my job review by saying, "We're not happy." I said, "Very few people who work here are."

The boss said, "We find your work wanting." I said, "Good. Then it matches my salary."

My job evaluation was so bad that I couldn't do any work for the rest of the week. Fortunately, nobody noticed the difference.

JOB INTERVIEWS

It's easy to tell if a job interview goes well. You're confident beforehand and employed afterwards.

The tricks to a successful job interview are confidence, charm, and the ability to back up all the lies you put in your résumé.

A good job interview is one in which you are put on the hot seat and don't get off it until your retirement party.

A job interview is a monumental moment. It's the last time you'll ever hear your boss say, "Sit back and relax."

Helpful Hint: When the interviewer asks, "Where would you like to be in 5 years?" "Lying on a beach in Bermuda" isn't the correct answer.

The job applications are not prepared properly. In the space marked "Sex" I had a difficult time writing small enough to respond, "Certainly, but never during working hours."

LATENESS

One coworker is always late. If you're not at work before him, there's no sense in coming.

We call him West Coast because he's always 3 hours behind the rest of us.

He has a special alarm clock. When it goes off, it doesn't ring and doesn't buzz. It just says, "The hell with it!" and throws itself out the window.

The boss told this gentleman once, "You're supposed to be here by 8 o'clock in the morning." His response was, "Wow. You mean there's an 8 o'clock in the morning, too?"

The boss said, "If you're late tomorrow, you're fired." He said, "Why don't you fire me today? Then I can't be late tomorrow."

He's late for everything. He was 3 months old when he was born.

He's late for everything. Every year he wins the best Halloween costume contest at the office Christmas party.

He once owned a pet rooster that crowed every day at the crack of noon.

One day the boss asked him, "Do you know what time we start work in this office?" This guy said, "Oh, you're never here in time to find out, either?"

The boss told him once, "You know everyone else in this office is hard at work at 8 o'clock." He said, "Yeah, I know. That's why I'm very careful not to come in at that time and disturb them."

The boss talked to this gentleman and said, "What can I possibly do to absolutely guarantee that you won't be late for work tomorrow morning?" He said, "Give me the day off."

This worker was the champion latecomer of all time. It took him 42 years to earn his 25-year pin.

This guy is tardy for everything. He wrote into his will that if he's late for his funeral, he wants the pallbearers to start without him.

He was late for his own wedding. The bride and the best man were 3 days into the honeymoon before he arrived.

LONG LUNCHES

The boss asked one worker, "What time did you get back from lunch?" The employee said, "Oh, about a quarter of twelve." The boss said, "I saw you coming in at 3 o'clock." The worker said, "Well, three is a quarter of twelve, isn't it?"

After a long lunch one employee looked at his watch and said, "I'd better get back to the office." The other said, "Yeah, you'd hate to miss your retirement party."

Some executives take extra-long lunches. They can't tell the difference between doing business for the company and giving the company the business.

That's why they put names on the executives' doors—so when they come back from those long lunches, they'll remember which office to go into.

The boss said to one returning executive, "You left for lunch a long time ago." The employee said, "How long?" The boss said, "Three mergers ago."

Some executives get confused. They keep getting "lunch time" mixed up with "leave of absence."

One executive came back from lunch even later than usual. He thought the boss would be mad, but he was quite pleasant. He said, "I hope you enjoyed your vacation."

One executive I know enjoys several martinis with his long lunches. In fact, he doesn't call it lunch time; he calls it "bobbing for olives."

One executive asked his secretary, "What do I have scheduled from Tuesday to Thursday next week?" His secretary said, "Lunch."

One executive said to the boss, "I'm going to lunch now." The boss said, "Try to come back while your tie is still in style, will you?"

I know one executive who takes such long lunches and has so many martinis during them that when he returns he has to check the management organizational chart to find out which one he is.

You know you're taking too long when quitting time keeps interrupting the best part of your lunch.

My boss said to his secretary, "I'm going out to lunch." The secretary said, "Fine. I'll alert the Missing Persons Bureau."

The boss said to his secretary, "I'm going to lunch now." The secretary said, "Where can I reach you in case any of your children graduate?"

MEAN BOSS

I have a mean boss. He has a pinup over his desk. It's a nude photo of the Wicked Witch of the East.

My boss is so mean he only gives out sick leave posthumously.
. . . he wants to be sure you're really sick.
. . . anything earlier than that he figures is malingering.

My boss is so tough he has a black belt in management.

He's so mean that if he were made warden of a Turkish prison, he would consider it a lateral move.

Of course, he never would be offered that job—warden of a Turkish prison. He's overqualified.

Nobody likes my boss. He only gets one Christmas card a year.
. . . it's from his mother.
. . . telling him not to come to the family Christmas dinner.

He's a vicious man. When he reads the story of the Pied Piper, he roots for the rats.
. . . it's a form of professional courtesy.

I have a very unlikable boss. He has the personality of the Hong Kong Flu.

My boss's annual physical includes a heart exam. He has to rent one for the day.

MEETINGS

"He's in a meeting" is business*ese* for "Sure he's here, but why would he want to talk to you?"

A lot of meetings are where a bunch of people have nothing to do, so they decide to do it together.

I heard an executive say, "I don't feel much like working today. I don't know whether to go home early or call a meeting."

I never take notes at meetings. I figure any meeting that I'm invited to can't be about anything that important.

A coworker takes lots of notes at meetings. It gives the impression he understands what's going on.

Many business meetings are just a waste of time with an agenda.

Some business meetings are a whole bunch of nothing with a big table in the middle.

An executive asked his secretary, "Do I have any meetings scheduled for today?" The secretary said, "No." He said, "Then what am I doing here?"

One executive had so many meetings scheduled that he couldn't make them all. He discovered he got more done at the ones he missed.

At one meeting we all had a blank note pad in front of us along with a copy of the agenda. We spent the first 10 minutes of the meeting figuring out which was which.

The most productive thing to come out of today's meeting was the adjournment.

I love closed-door meetings. Especially when the doors are closed without me being in the room.

MEMOS

If you say absolutely nothing, it's called silence. If you write absolutely nothing, it's called a memo.

If it weren't for the mailing list attached, some memos would contain no information at all.

Boiled down to its basics, a memo is saying "Here's some useless information I thought you might find useful."

When someone asks for a memo, they're really saying, "I don't have time to ignore you now. Send me a memo so that I can ignore you later."

A memo is interoffice junk mail.

The boss asked, "Did you get my memo?" I said, "I read your memo, but I didn't get it."

I got a memo from my boss saying he'd like to totally eliminate office memos.
. . . so I sent a memo back saying I agreed with him.

I've found with most interoffice memos, once you say "From" and "To" you've pretty much said it all.

I save all the interoffice memos I receive. It's cheaper than scratch paper.

I hate memos that start "From the desk of . . ." I don't like office furniture giving me orders.

Most memos that start with "From the desk of . . ." should really start with "To the wastebasket of . . ."

When a memo is stamped "Important," that means it should get special attention. It should be thrown away before any others.

My boss has an interesting philosophy: If you can't say anything nice, send a memo.

Memos are quick communications that are designed to be read and thrown away, but not necessarily in that order.

One good thing about memos: I once worked at a company for 10 years and had wonderful communication with my employees, and not once did I ever have to look at any of them.

Some memos are silly. My boss passed out a 2-page memo to every one of the 500 employees. The memo said, "Don't waste paper."

OFFICE COFFEE

The coffee in our office is so bad that Dr. Jack Kevorkian recommends it to all his patients.

The coffee in our office is so strong that you can have it by the cup or by the slice.

The coffee is bad, but they say you get used to it. That's because after 3 or 4 days, it eats away your taste buds.

The coffee is so strong. There's only one person in our office who doesn't drink coffee. He's easy to spot. He's the one who still blinks.

We have a secret office recipe for our coffee. It reads: "Take whatever was left in the pot from yesterday and reheat it."

It's real company coffee. It wakes you up on Monday morning and keeps you awake until Friday.

This coffee will put hair on your chest. What happens is: Your eyebrows fall out and drop down.

The coffee they brew in our office is unbelievable. Unbelievable in the sense of "hard to swallow."

It's very strong coffee. We found out it can remove nail polish . . . up to the second joint.

A new employee came into our office and said, "I'd love to have a cup of coffee." Someone asked, "One lump or two?" She said, "I don't take sugar." The employee said, "Who said anything about sugar?"

OFFICE COLLECTIONS

They take up so many collections in our office it's hurting production. It's hard to get any work done with one hand always in your pocket.

In some offices they pass the hat. In our office they take cash, checks, or credit cards.

They're always collecting for something. Last time, I said, "What's this donation for?" They said, "Nothing. We just didn't want you to get out of practice."

One guy in our office takes up so many collections that his hand is permanently shaped like a cigar box.

Sneeze in our office and you get a get-well gift before you get a *"Gesundheit."*

I'm always giving money to some cause or another. Working in this office is like having a child in college.

They're always asking for money to get a gift for someone. They call it the Sunshine Club. I call it extortion.

It's just like highway robbery, except you get to sign the card.

Our office is always asking for more money from us. They must be confused. They think they're the government.

It's the most money I've ever put in a collection basket without at least getting to sing a hymn.

I think it would be cheaper for me if I quit this place and started working in an office full of pickpockets.

Finally, I got disgusted and said, "I have nothing left to give." So they took up a collection for me since I was down on my luck.

OFFICE FEUDS

Our office is like one big family—which means there are always eight or nine feuds going on.

There are so many feuds going on in our office that the vending machine comes with a food taster.

Nobody talks to anybody else in our office. We have to call a truce to get a rumor started.

I don't get along with anybody in our office. At the company picnic, I hang out with the ants.

There are so many feuds in our office that at the end of the day you can either punch the time clock or anyone standing near it.

Our boss wasn't talking to his secretary. He had to dictate his letters to her in pantomine.

Two deskmates just made up the other day. One said, *"Gesundheit."* The other said, "What was that for?" The first one said, "You sneezed 7 years ago, but I wasn't talking to you at the time."

Our secretary's not talking to the boss. He gets all his phone messages by mail.

Nobody in our office talks to anybody else. They growl occasionally, but don't talk.

There are a lot of feuds in our office. We not only have a janitorial service, but twice a week we have a minesweeper come in and do the aisles.

In our office, back stabbing is considered a job skill.

We keep a book in the office called *How to Win Friends and Influence People.* We throw it at each other occasionally.

OFFICE GOSSIP

There's plenty of gossip in our office. The rule of thumb is: if someone's not talking *to* you, they're talking *about* you.

We don't need air-conditioning in our office. The wagging tongues keep it cool enough.

Gossip: that's telling a story that might be true so often that it becomes true.

Some people love gossip. They say, "Do you realize how dull life would be if we had to rely only on the truth?"

Some people in our office want to keep a secret so badly that they tell it to someone else so that they can help them keep it.

One gossip told me a tale that she swore was true. She said, "Would I have made up that story in the first place if it wasn't true?"

Folks love gossip. As one coworker said, "I know that's a false rumor, but it's just too juicy not to believe."

Yes, sir . . . the best way to get a memo read in our office is to distribute it in the form of a rumor.

I asked another gossip if a story he told me was true. He said, "Most of it is. I had to add some of the bad parts just to get people to listen."

I asked another gossip if a story he told was true. He said, "Of course it's not. I wouldn't stoop to telling the truth about my friends."

The best stories to tell someone are the ones that begin, "Please don't tell this to anyone, but . . ."

One gossip in our office spreads stories so fast that his tongue has a racing stripe down the middle of it.

OFFICE INEFFICIENCY

Our office is so inefficient that calling it "the workplace" is a contradiction in terms.

Our office is just a social club with a manager.

We used to have one worker in our office, but a quick petition got rid of him.

If anything in our office absolutely has to get done, we farm it out to less fortunate employees.

Some weeks we get absolutely nothing done; other weeks less.

Our office is so inefficient you'd think that most of us who work there were elected.

When the people in our office say, "I'm going to work," they're lying.

On the company organizational chart our department is represented by a question mark.

When they closed our office for renovations, production actually went up.

Our workers are so inefficient that in our office, absenteeism is encouraged.
. . . it's the only way to get any work done.

We had one job that had to be completed in 5 business days, and no one in our office knew what they were.

The vending machine in our office doesn't work, and it doesn't seem at all out of place.

OFFICE PARTY

Always keep your mouth full of food at the office party. It's better to weigh too much than say too much.

Always stay sober at the office party. Remembering what you said is preferable to hoping someone else will forget what you don't remember saying.

The office party is an excellent time for good friends to gather together and complain about one another.

At one office party, I complained to someone that the boss never listens to me. Unfortunately, it was the boss listening to me at the time.

Be careful what you say to whom at office parties. All coworkers look the same when their faces are blurry.
. . . or when your mind is.

You know you had too much fun at the office party when the boss leaves a note on your desk that says, "Be in my office at 9 this morning, and bring the punch bowl that you wore home last night."

You know you had too much fun at the office party when you show up for work and find that your desk is being dusted for fingerprints.

You know you had too much fun at the office party when none of your coworkers show up for work the next morning, . . . but all of their lawyers do.

You know you had too much fun at the office party when you show up for work the next morning, and you can't get into your parking space because your desk is there.

You know you had too much fun at the office party when you get fired the following morning, and you can't remember ever working there.

You know you had too much fun at the office party when you're late for work the following morning because it took you an extra long time in the shower trying to get all the tar and feathers off.

OFFICE SUPPLIES

They're very tight with office supplies in our office. If you need a legal pad, it's easier to hire a lawyer and borrow one from him.

They guard office supplies diligently where I work. There are paper clips in our office that have more seniority than I have.

They collect old desk calendars in our office. It seems silly now, but if 1986 ever rolls around again, they'll save a bundle.

You have to fill out a formal request form for everything you want. What they save in supplies, they spend on printing up formal request forms.

They try not to waste any supplies. Doodling in our office is a felony.

My office has a system. When you run out of an item, you simply fill out a requisition form and give it to the office manager. This works well unless, of course, it's requisition forms you run out of.

I got an automatic stapler in my office. You fill it up, plug it in, turn it on, and staple. Before it used to take me 2 seconds to staple pages together. Now it takes me 8 minutes.
. . . 12 if I don't have the manual handy.

My boss told us we shouldn't waste office supplies. Of course, he told us this as he was making a replica of the Eiffel Tower out of paper clips.

In our office, the supplies are kept in a locked closet. It's nice to know that if a burglar breaks in, he can get the computers, the fax machines, and the copiers, but the boxes of Kleenex are safe.

Paper clips are a lot like relatives. They're always around until you actually need one.

I have 36 ball-point pens in my desk drawer. Someday I have to go through them and find out which is the one that still writes.

PARKING SPACE

I take the bus to work so that none of my coworkers will know what a lousy parking space I have.

My parking space is so bad, it's not worth buying a car for.

It's pretty far away from the office. The nice thing about my parking space is that by the time I get to my car after work, I'm halfway home.

Our company has moved three times, but I've still got the same parking space.

My parking space is so far away from the office that I put on more mileage each year than my car does.

My parking spot is so far away from the office that we're not sure whether it's a parking space or a branch office.

My parking space is to our office what Hawaii is to the mainland.

If our office were a map of the United States, my parking space would be Madagascar.

They asked if I wanted my name painted on my parking space. I refused. I don't mind the walk so much, but I couldn't take the humiliation.

My parking space is just on the legal limit. If it were ten more yards from the office, they'd have to pay me a per diem.

My parking space is closer to my home than to my office.

The nice thing about having a lousy parking space is that nobody ever steals it.

That's why they have to give me 2 weeks' notice before they fire me. They have to allow me time enough to get to my car.

RÉSUMÉ

A résumé is a list of all the things you've done so well that you're not doing them anymore.

A résumé is one sheet of fiction writing in search of a happy ending.

Do you realize that résumés would look a lot different if they were written under oath?

Résumés are a series of white lies written on a sheet of white paper.

A good résumé is a double-edged sword. Would you really want to work for anybody who was dumb enough to believe yours?

It's pretty depressing to realize the most interesting parts of the résumé you've written are the margins.

Don't tell me you can't put your résumé on one side of one sheet of paper. They got Nolan Ryan's entire career on a bubble-gum card.

There's a company now that writes superb résumés for anyone seeking employment. It's called Lies-Я-Us.

Don't put too many embellishments on your résumé. Remember, you may be asked to deliver it in person.

I think I did too good a job on my résumé. The guy in the Personnel Office said, "We don't hire people like this. We pray to them."

The personnel manager handed me back my résumé and said, "If you can bring us someone who fits this description, we'll pay you a finder's fee."

I showed up at the Personnel Office and the manager said, "I've read your résumé. Is there some reason why you've decided not to wear your halo today?"

The guy at the employment agency said, "I loved your résumé. Someday I'd like to meet the person it's about."

The personnel manager said, "We've checked the facts on your résumé. If this was an alibi, you'd be in jail now."

After I wrote my résumé, it was so unimpressive it convinced me to keep working for the salary I was making.

RETIREMENT

Retirement: You've been doing nothing for the company for years. Now it's time to do it for yourself.

Retirement: This is the time when your spouse finally finds out what your coworkers have been putting up with for years.

Here at the company you had supervisors, managers, executive managers, vice-presidents, and the CEO. At home, you'll just have your spouse. Now you'll learn what following orders really means.

As you retire from the company, we know you're not going home alone. You're probably taking a few office supplies with you.

We have mixed emotions at retirements. We know we're losing a valued coworker and good friend, but we're gaining a parking space.

We know that retirement is a time for relaxation and fun. Frankly, though, it's hard to picture you any more relaxed than you were at work.

Racehorses retire to stud. To our guest-of-honor I say: Don't even think about it.

Now that you're retired, you're going to have to find things to do to keep yourself busy. For the past few months we've had a helluva time doing that for you here at work.

Now that you're retired, you can hunt and fish and go for walks in the woods. For you, that's called golf.

I asked your wife what your retirement meant to her. She said, "It probably means just one more thing around the house that has to be dusted."

Now that you're retired, you'll have to find yourself a fun little hobby that you can tinker with now and again when you get bored. Before you retired, that was your work.

Someone once said, "You have to plan to do things during your retirement. You can't just sit around the house all day and do nothing." It was my spouse who said that.

You have to plan retirement activities—choose something that doesn't cost too much while you're doing it or hurt too much after you've done it.

You have to plan some activity for your retirement—golf, fishing, anything but spending.

There's one good thing about retirement. Even if you don't do it well, you can't get fired.

One gentleman complained, "I retired with about one-quarter of my salary . . . or roughly about what I was worth when I was working there."

Retirement doesn't mean good-bye. You can still hang around with your coworkers and visit with fellow employees here at work. You're just not going to get paid for it.
. . . I guess that *does* mean good-bye.

Racehorses are retired to stud. Unfortunately, that's not one of the options on our pension plan.

I'm happy to say I retired from active business 5 years ago. The company makes it official tomorrow.

The boss said at my retirement party, "We were going to hold this retirement at your desk, but it's been so long since there's been any activity there . . ."

SALARY

The boss said, "I pay you a living wage." I said, "That's not living; it's existing."

I finally figured out why I'm having trouble making ends meet. The company pays me a salary that's so small, it only has one end to it.

What I can't figure out is: Since the government takes half my salary, how come they don't drive me to work every other week.

The boss said, "There's a little something in your pay envelope this week." It was my pay.

I told the boss to pay me what I'm worth. He said, "I wouldn't have anybody working here for that little."

The boss said, "You get a day's pay for a day's work." I said, "Yeah, but it doesn't pay a day's expenses."

You know what I have left after I pay my taxes and my expenses? More taxes and more expenses.

I can make it on my salary. That leaves my wife and kids to fend for themselves.

It seems that every time I get a 5-percent raise, I get 10 percent more responsibility.

My last promotion was a new job title, not a salary increase. So now my debtors are owed money by a more important person.

At my last review the boss said, "We're not going to give you a salary increase, but we are giving you a new job title." I called him a few new things, too.

The boss told me that to a devoted employee, money was not important. I said, "If it's so unimportant, give me more of it."

SCHEDULING

A completion date is not a date when a project will be completed. It's a date after which you have to furnish excuses for why it's not completed.

God built the world in 6 days, but He wasn't depending on independent contractors.

The boss said, "I want this job done right, and I want it by Friday." I said, "Make up your mind."

The boss said, "Can you have this project on my desk by Friday?" I said, "Sure. That'll give you the whole weekend to finish it for me."

The boss said, "I'm giving you 2 days to complete this project." I said, "Good. I'll take April 14th and July 27th."

I always plan each project precisely and meticulously. It's the only way I can know exactly how much I'm not doing.

I've never been behind schedule in my life. Of course, I do waste a lot of valuable time making up revised schedules.

The customer complained, "You promised to have this job done in record time, and now you're 3 months late." I said, "Well, isn't that a record?"

My customer said, "You promised you'd have this job completed this week. You gave me your word." I said, "Yeah, but I didn't tell you that word was 'sorry.'"

The boss kept pestering me to finish this job. Finally he said, "What's holding this project up?" I said, "You."

I told the boss it would take me 8 days to complete this project. He said, "Eight days? I could travel around the world in that time." I said, "If you do that, I can have it done in five."

The boss said, "I want you to complete this project in 3 days." I said, "If I do, then neither I nor the project will be worth a damn."

SMOKING VS. NONSMOKING

They put up a sign in our office that read, "Thank You for Not Smoking." Someone rolled it up and smoked it.

To counter secondhand smoke in our office, everyone glares at you with firsthand dirty looks.

Our office is very adamant about not smoking. They've hired Smokey the Bear as a security guard.

. . . three or four whacks from his shovel and you're a non-smoker for life.

At our office you're invited to step outside to enjoy a smoke. The problem is, we're on the 16th floor.

. . . but you can pretty much finish a cigarette on the way down.

One guy I know is a chain-smoker. I asked him why. He said he's heard too much about how harmful secondhand smoke is, so he's trying to keep his lungs filled with firsthand smoke.

Nonsmokers are very militant in our office. If you light up, they'll use a fire extinguisher on you. Not to squirt it at you; to hit you over the head with it.

One nonsmoker berated a smoker in our office. The smoker asked, "Do you really believe smoking can shorten my life?" The nonsmoker said, "I absolutely do, because if you light that cigarette, I'm gonna kill you."

It used to be that everybody smoked and our office was constantly filled with secondhand smoke. It got so that the only way you could stay healthy was to take a sick day.

They caught one guy smoking in our office, and everyone chastised him terribly. It wasn't even his fault. His pacemaker shorted out.

We have a designated smoking area in our office. It's called New Jersey.

STATUS OFFICE

A high-status office in our company is one with an outside window. I'm still trying to get an office with a door.

My office doesn't have an outside window, but it comes close. It only has three walls.

My boss has an office with an outside window, and he's still not satisfied. Now he wants a stained-glass window.

My boss is real status-conscious. It's discouraging to go into his office and sit in a chair that is worth more to the company than I am.

My boss has a very large office, but he can't use it all the time. His kids use it on weekends to play soccer games.

A large office is a sure sign of status. My office would seem larger if they didn't insist on keeping brooms, mops, and buckets in there, too.

I've always wanted an office with my own private restroom. I finally got it, but now I need to have exact change any time I want to go into it.

My boss's office is so large, there are two desks sitting outside it—one for his secretary and one for the tour guide.

My boss's office is so large it can comfortably sleep ten . . . which makes it perfect for staff meetings.

His desk is enormous. Meeting with him is like trying to converse with a man who's hiding behind an aircraft carrier.

If you take just one of the drawers from his desk and put a table and chair in there, you have my office.

He has a picture on the corner of his desk, but it's so far away from him that he can't tell if it's his family or not.

UNTIDY DESK

My desk is the untidiest in the world. In fact, the desk that is the second most untidy is probably lost somewhere on the top of my desk.

I cleaned my desk once and found three employees we thought had retired.

I do a lot of work at home. I have to. At work, there's no room on my desk left to do it.

The last time I cleaned my desk, the stuff was so old I just threw it all out, although I did sell 6 magazines to my doctor for his waiting room.

I've got so many coffee stains on my desk top, Juan Valdez wants to buy it for his museum.

I call my desk David Copperfield, because everything you put on it disappears.

My untidy desk is a form of job security. If they ever tell me to clean out my desk and go home, that should take me well into my retirement years.

In a way, it's a rather clean desk. There's no room on it for dust.

It's an environmentally aware desk. As long as my desk top has as much junk on it as it does now, silverfish will never become an endangered species.

I never really clean my desk, but every few months I at least try to rid it of things that are moving.

Some employees sit at their desks and worry about termination. I worry about an avalanche.

I not only can't find a phone message on my desk; I can't find the phone.

VACATION

Vacations are depressing when you stop to think that it takes just 2 weeks to spend what you've been saving all year for.

It's demoralizing to realize that 50 weeks of work are financially equal to 2 weeks of vacation.

I spent my entire vacation just lying on the beach wondering if I could afford this.

My family is very easy to please when it comes to vacation spots. They like any place that I can't afford.

Vacation is a time we take out of our schedules each year to remind us how easy work really is, in comparison.

Why is it when I return from a 2-week vacation that 6 weeks of work has piled up on my desk?

Vacations are tough. After a 2-week vacation with my family, it takes me about 50 weeks of work to rest up for the next one.

Vacations are supposed to be a break from work. But most vacation spots are so expensive now that a working person can't afford them.

On our first day at the resort my kids said, "There's nothing to do here." I said, "Do it anyway. It's costing me $300 a day."

Each person in our family wanted to go to a different place for vacation. Now that's what I call a real vacation.

I did absolutely nothing on my vacation except go fishing every single day. I had to. On our first day there, my wallet fell into the stream.

My wife and I finally went on a budget cruise that was within our price range, but we had to cut it short. On the third day out, her hands got blisters from rowing.

Index

About the Author

Gene Perret was born in Philadelphia, Pennsylvania, and he worked there for 13 years in General Electric's switchgear plant in the electrical drafting and engineering departments.

He began his comedy-writing and speaking career by emceeing company banquets and parties. His hobby became a full-time profession in 1969, when he left GE to write for Bob Hope, Phyllis Diller, Carol Burnett, Tim Conway, and for many other stars and shows. He has collected three Emmy awards for writing and one Writers Guild Award, among other accolades, along the way.

Mr. Perret has traveled extensively with Bob Hope, including command performances for King Gustav of Sweden and for the 25th anniversary of the coronation of Queen Elizabeth II of Great Britain. He also was the only writer to journey into war zones of Beirut, Lebanon; the Persian Gulf; and Saudi Arabia with Mr. Hope's U.S.O. Christmas tours.

Today, Mr. Perret performs his own brand of after-dinner humor for many associations and corporations across the country. He also writes a monthly humor column for *Arizona Highways* and contributes articles to magazines like *Reader's Digest*, *Good Housekeeping*, *Parenting*, *Friends*, and *Toastmaster*.

Mr. Perret and his wife, Joanne, live near Los Angeles. Their four children—Joe, Terry, Carole, and Linda—are grown and on their own; so, they concentrate on spoiling their two grandsons, Michael and Brett, and their granddaughter, Sophia.